Understanding Interfaith:

THE WHAT, WHY, AND WHO

Clive Johnson

labyrinthe

Copyright © 2017 by Clive Johnson.

First published September 2017.

All rights reserved. No part of this publication may be reproduced, distributed or transmitted in any form or by any means, including photocopying, recording, or other electronic or mechanical methods, without the prior written permission of the publisher, except in the case of brief quotations embodied in critical reviews and certain other noncommercial uses permitted by copyright law.

Labyrinthe Press
Leigh-on-Sea, United Kingdom
www.labyrinthepublishers.com

Book Layout©2017 BookDesignTemplates.com
Cover illustration ©iStock/franckreporter
Distributed by CreateSpace

British Library Cataloguing in Publication Data
Understanding Interfaith/Clive Johnson. –1st ed.
ISBN 978-1-9997885-0-6 (print edition)
ISBN 978-1-9997885-1-3 (electronic edition)

Also available as an Audible digital audiobook.

Quantity sales. Special discounts may be obtained on quantity purchases of this book. For details, please contact info@labyrinthepublishers.com.

Contents

Preface 5
Why the big fuss? 15
What is Interfaith? 23
Where is the common ground? 41
How are interfaith perspectives being expressed? 65
How should we respond? 89
Notes 103
References 105
Terminology 113
Bibliography 119
The Interfaith Resources Guide 124

Clive Johnson

"We must acknowledge (others) who they are in all their integrity, with their conscientiously held beliefs; we must welcome them and respect them as who they are and walk reverently on what is their holy ground, taking off our shoes, metaphorically and literally... We must hold to our particular and peculiar beliefs tenaciously, not pretending that all religions are the same... We must be ready to learn from one another, not claiming that we alone possess all truth and that somehow we have a corner on God."

— Archbishop Desmond Tutu[1]

"The religions of the world are expressions of the human openness to God. They are signs of God's presence in the world. Every religion is unique, and through this uniqueness, religions enrich each other. In their specificity, they manifest different faces of the supreme mystery which is never exhausted. In diversity, they enable us to experience the richness of the One more profoundly. When religions encounter one another in dialogue, they build up a community in which differences become complementarities and divergences are changed into pointers to communion."

—Indian Theological Association[2]

Clive Johnson

"In the twenty-first century we will see social and political landscapes across the globe continue to change; new cultural and intellectual trends will give unexpected color and dimension to old ideas; scientific and technological innovations will surprise us with new opportunities to flourish and new problems that we must try to solve. Religious and spiritual people are already coming together, despite differences and historical antagonism, to guide our changing world toward justice, peace, and sustainability. In the next century, religious and spiritual diversity need not persist as a source of conflict, but can instead emerge as a potent source of hope"

— State of Interreligious Movement Report June 2008[3]

Preface

I AM AN ORDAINED interfaith minister. When I introduce myself as such to people that I've not met before, very few claim that they've not heard about interfaith ministry before. The term 'interfaith' seems to be in vogue in my part of the world, even if after shaking my hand, many are inclined to ask me– "so what *exactly* do you do?"

My primary motivation for writing this book is an attempt to reply to this very reasonable question. I also hope to offer a response to two common follow-on questions–"what does the interfaith movement (or ministry) aim to achieve?" and, more fundamentally, "what does the term 'interfaith' actually mean?"

My usual response to these questions is to suggest that interfaith recognizes that there are many diverse ways for individuals to express their spiritual selves and to connect with what is sacred, while my task is to help those who come to me to relate to this in whatever way is most meaningful for them.

But of course, this simple offering begs further questions about what I mean by 'spiritual,' 'the sacred,' 'The Divine,' and more. Hence, the need for a little more considered exploration.

In our multicultural world, people from different faith backgrounds rub shoulders more than ever before. Furthermore, there is now a far greater proportion of people than perhaps at any other time in history who don't align themselves with any particular religious tradition, including many millions who nonetheless see themselves as being 'spiritual.'

It should then perhaps not be surprising that something should emerge to fill the gap in situations where folks from different faith backgrounds or who express their spiritual lives in different ways want to be married, but who may feel alienated from doing so in a setting that's only in keeping with one of their traditions. But this raises the question–what might this 'something' look like?

Should this be something that attempts to blend aspects of what might often appear to be the various ways of honouring God (or many gods)–something that might find some common ground, but not gets to the nub of what is important for either? Should it rather be something that dispels with the teachings and practices of the established faith traditions altogether, or at least with the rituals and liturgies practised by the majority of religious institutions? Or is it perhaps something completely new–a response to the desire of many people for a place or community that allows them to express their spirituality, but that doesn't require them to be confined to a particular box, or to practise what most people would describe as being 'religious'?

I believe that the concept of interfaith can apply to all of these, and more. It's a term that has alternative meanings for different people, and is one that can't be easily pinned down to a single definition. Paradoxically, to have an interfaith mindset doesn't mean that you can't still be a staunch follower of a particular faith tradition–and with this, having strong beliefs about life and death, notions of whatever is meant by having a 'soul,' and Who or What God is.

My journey is not untypical of those who've come to value having an interfaith mindset. I was brought up to be a good Christian boy–going to Sunday school when I was young, and later soaking up everything that the close-knit evangelical church that I attended as an adult could offer me. I studied my Bible, and diligently prayed every night, reverently and superstitiously. I felt touched by the Holy Spirit, and never doubted the truth of the words that were spoken from the pulpit. I genuinely believed that Jesus was my saviour, and I defended this view with a passion whenever I was challenged about it.

Something happened during my 30s and 40s—I can't now remember exactly what—that took me away from being a regular churchgoer for several years. But, despite occasional periods of doubt, I didn't give up on my belief that God is real and felt sure that the way that I conducted my life would be all important when it came to earning my place on the 'right side' after I passed on. I wanted to make sure that I didn't rule myself out from enjoying the promised bliss of eternal salvation. For me, this meant aligning with the one true God, with what I saw as being the only true way to get to heaven.

However, something was changing for me, even if this shift was occurring very subtly and in ways that I wasn't always aware of. My tendency to accept whatever I was told about matters of faith without questioning was beginning to lessen, and gradually, I began to take an interest in the teachings of other faiths.

To my surprise, I was quite drawn to many of them—I loved the idea of following the flow of the Tao, and saw great wisdom in the teachings of Buddha. I discovered that the warm, uplifting, and unifying spirit that accompanied *kirtan* [1] singing was no different to the touching presence that I'd often experienced in Christian worship. The exquisitely beautiful Suras of The *Qur'an* could move me no less than could reading a verse from the Bible. I began to appreciate that the rituals and practices of Eastern and other faith traditions–which had before seemed to me very far removed from the pious, 'holy' practices of the Anglican Church with which I was familiar–were no less lacking in meaning and sacredness.

So it was that I began to explore ideas held by people of different faiths, and began joining in a number of their activities–and not just the 'big six' religions [2], but some of the lesser known ones too.

I started reading widely and ultimately came to a point where I wanted to set about a course of study that would allow me to pursue my exploration further. This course–in interfaith ministry–would take me on a journey of personal development that I couldn't have imagined. But this was just one part of my waking up to the wonderfully diverse ways in which people make sense of their spirituality, and coming to an appreciation of how others perceive their purpose and place in the world.

Stories of past and inter-life regression, the esoteric teachings of esteemed early twentieth century teachers such as Rudolf Steiner and George Gurdjieff, and reports of near-death experiences and the like all added wonder to my inquiry. Powerful metaphors found in mythology, and the striking truths that are to be found in many classic fairy tales were later to play a part in this, as were some of the teachings of the Swiss psychologist Carl Jung, philosophers such as Dante and Immanuel Kant, and my occasional novice's dip into the mysteries of quantum physics.

Being welcomed at mosques, Hindu temples, and synagogues contributed to my education. So too did a daily practice of meditation, and having some exposure–at least for a short while–to a variety of spiritual practices (Tai Ch'i, kundalini yoga, shamanic journeying, and more).

What was becoming clear to me at an intuitive level was that the breadth of what I was learning and experiencing was helping me come into touch with my true self, increasing my awareness of my soul's voice and my nature as a spiritual being. Nothing that I encountered seemed to contradict anything else that my inquiry was revealing.

The thirty or more souls who came to train as Interfaith Ministers at the same time as I came from many different backgrounds–agnostics and followers of the Tarot, spiritualists and Sufis, Rastafarians and individuals whose Roman Catholic or Anglican upbringing had left them with many scars, practising Buddhists and enthusiastic Christian evangelicals. The human faces that made up our circle transcended many boundaries of colour, ethnicity, geographical home, and sexual identity.

Individually, we had all reached a point where we recognized that we had far more in common than that which separated us. Together, we grew to understand that we were all intimately united, and that however we individually made sense of our relationship with The Divine, there really is only one Great Spirit, Creator, the Cosmos, Mother Earth, Absolute, or however each of us preferred to conceive the essence or power that is the source of all life.

Appreciating that individuals from different backgrounds have an opportunity to hear the same truths makes it easier to answer questions such as the one that atheists often pose to Christians–for those who've never heard the message of the gospels, how can it be fair that they don't have an opportunity to be saved?

"You're quite correct," would now be my reply. "It doesn't seem fair. But perhaps those people have an approach to find the same God, but in their way."

Such a response might not sit well with many Christians, but is one example of where I've parted company with the mindset that I once had.

It makes perfect sense to me that, in a world that has been constantly evolving, there would be many ways in which God would want to communicate with people from different cultures, not to mention the millions of tribes, communities, and societies that have come and gone over the many thousands' of years in human history, who have never had an opportunity to hear the Christian story.

Adopting an interfaith perspective allows us to appreciate that there is more than one way for important lessons or truths to be communicated. For example, should we assume that the message that accompanies the story of the Israelites' exodus from Egypt–that those who follow God will be saved and reunited with Him–is any different from the message of the New Testament? Personally, I believe that there is no fundamental difference in teaching here.

However, to acquire such a perspective isn't usually just a case of recognizing the common threads that appear in the texts of different traditions through a study of comparative religion, but also by having a comprehension that comes from the heart.

Each faith has a mystical tradition—a level of understanding of its teachings that may in some cases be passed on in secret and through lengthy apprenticeships in its wisdom schools. This always involves 'going inside' (allowing the heart to speak), usually through deep meditation, separation from earthly comforts, and prayer.

It's through such practices that spiritual insight can be found. This is an understanding that comes directly from God and is one that doesn't involve any third party's intervention.

The interfaith inquiry is an exciting one for anyone who chooses to look beyond their current perspective. It's an invitation not just to engage in a dialogue with people of other faiths and to join in shared activities with them, but to deepen our understanding of our worldview. It's therefore one that I believe is critically important to embrace.

A note about terminology

I should say a word about the terminology that I've adopted in this book.

I offer definitions for several common terms in an appendix at the back of the book. These are descriptions that I have applied, not necessarily definitive or universally accepted ones. As such, the appendix serves as an explanation of what the terms mean as they are used in this text.

I've also adopted the common convention to use title case (capitalizing the first letters) for honorific terms like God, Source, *The Holy Qur'an*, and The Absolute, as well as associated pronouns (She, He, They, It, etc). I intend no gender or other bias when using such markers.

Clive Johnson

CHAPTER 1

Why the big fuss?

"Nobody fully comprehends what religion is who imagines that his own religion is the only genuine religion."

— Josiah Royce[1].

"We should in humility and joyfulness acknowledge that the supernatural and divine reality we all worship in some form or other transcends all our particular categories of thought and imagining...We should seek to share all insights we can and be ready to learn, for instance, from the techniques of the spiritual life that are available in religions other than our own."

—Archbishop Desmond Tutu[2].

Clive Johnson

"Dialogue between the faiths is a necessity. This necessity springs from our experience that the world has become a global neighbourhood...But it is not just proximity that should persuade [us] into inter-faith dialogue.... As the offspring of God, we are in a direct sibling relationship with people of other faiths. It is as brothers and sisters in faith that we share in our common searching for God."

—Maxwell Craig[3].

FEW PEOPLE DISAGREE that encouraging a dialogue and promoting friendship among peoples of different faith traditions is a good thing. There have been many initiatives in recent years aimed at achieving this very end. Interfaith conferences have been held in locations around the world, multifaith music festivals have become annual fixtures in the calendars of some cities, and the leaders of different religious groups have joined to declare solidarity in the face of terrorist action, and to sign agreements in support of environmental and other causes of universal concern.

Even where such conversations aren't focused on how the world's religions can work together and recognizing the common principles that they abide by, any initiative that focuses on tolerating different points of view must surely be one to be encouraged.

Tolerance for the common man has a long-standing tradition in many faiths. In twelfth century Spain, for example, Jewish philosophers and Muslim clerics lived happily alongside one another. Buddhism, Hinduism, Jainism, and Taoism all have long histories of religious tolerance and respect for other faiths. The *Qur'an* expressly urges believers to treat followers of the other Abrahamic faiths as brothers: "Indeed, those who believed and those who were Jews or Christians or Sabaeans [before Prophet Muhammad]–those [among them] who believed in Allah and the Last Day and did righteousness–will have their reward with their Lord, and no fear will there be concerning them, nor will they grieve," (*Qur'an* 2.62, Sahih International translation).

The freedom to practice a chosen religion is enshrined in the United Nations Declaration of Human Rights, agreed to in 1948 by the then 58 member states [3].

Whether or not this provision is honoured in practice is of course another issue (as are, for that matter, several other articles of the same declaration). In part, the apparent ignoring of this agreement by some governments may stem from differing interpretations of what is meant by the concept of 'freedom.' In China and Japan for example, this is shaped by a widespread belief that human beings are considered to be entwined and interconnected with others, contrasting with the individualist mindset (individuals are self-contained and independent) that tends to dominate thinking in Western cultures.

The opposite of tolerance, of course, is a refusal to accept that anyone who doesn't share your particular point of view has the right to express and live according to that viewpoint. When spurred on by a teaching that advocates attacking those who don't share what is believed to be the 'true faith,' this can lead to conflict and violence. Wars motivated by religious differences have rarely taken a break over several millennia of recorded human history. And as is all too familiar, in recent years we have become acquainted with frequent examples of terrorist action claimed in the name of religion.

Against this backdrop, any attempt at an interfaith dialogue must be welcomed, while having tolerance for individuals who hold differing beliefs is a necessity. Better still, to be able to identify statements of belief that can be agreed upon, and finding ways to practise celebrating what can be shared by people of different faith backgrounds, should be reason enough to promote interfaith working as a vital concern for any civilised people. I believe that this is valuable not only at international, national and institutional levels, but in relationships between individuals as well.

Having a strong belief in anything that promotes questioning about what it means to be human, showing concern to our fellow man, and holding to such principles as being valuable guidance for life may be very desirable—a solid basis from which a person might grow in character, fulfil their potential, and feel motivated to share their gifts with others.

However, when a view that is passionately held becomes polarised against the perspective of another person, each individual must be careful to respect the other's viewpoints, avoiding the risk of falling into division, resentment, and entrenchment. Views that go to the heart of a person's value system have the power to split families, erode neighbourly relationships, and ultimately energise opposing sides that are ready to confront each other. This offers all the more reason, in my view, for individuals who hold a particular viewpoint of faith to seek to understand something of the perspectives of others.

If improving our knowledge of different faith systems is a good thing, possibly even extending to enjoying a common experience in praying, worshipping, or some other faith-based activity, then how might we go about developing our interfaith inquiry and engagement with others?

The approach taken in this book is to offer some entry points by exploring a variety of key questions—What are the different ways of conceiving what interfaith is about? What does someone who adopts an interfaith mindset believe? What is involved in people of different faith traditions (or who have no particular belief regarding matters of The Divine) coming together to find common ground? Is there a risk that someone who declares themselves to be 'spiritual' rather than 'religious,' or who adopts ideas from more than one tradition, might not find a grounding in anything in particular?

By exploring these and similar questions, my belief is that anyone who seeks to enhance their knowledge of the interfaith movement will discover a path of spiritual inquiry that is right for them.

In some cases, this may mean gaining a deeper appreciation of the teachings of the faith that they may hold at the moment, while at the same time coming to see others as not being so far removed in the way that they interpret the priorities for life. For others, it may encourage a path that loosens an adherence to a particular tradition. In each case, I'm sure that those who are open to learning about and better appreciating the worldviews of others will find their experience to be rewarding and inspiring.

I don't pretend to offer any more than an introduction to what is a topic that could be explored over many volumes, if not take many lifetimes to truly comprehend! There are many fine books and other sources of help for taking your inquiry further, several of which are listed in the appendix at the back of this book.

My intention is to offer something a little less ambitious– to demystify discussion of interfaith concepts, and to suggest some simple and accessible ways for engaging with the topic. My strongest recommendation is that having dipped a little into the breadth of questions and beginnings of answers that we will encounter, you may feel inclined to start exploring what grabs you in more detail, and, most beneficially, open yourself up to experiencing some spiritual practices of traditions that currently might be unfamiliar to you.

Clive Johnson

CHAPTER 2

What is Interfaith?

WHILE ACKNOWLEDGING the difficulties of arriving at a common understanding of what we mean when speaking about 'Interfaith,' a book that sets out to demystify this very conundrum must make a reasonable attempt to articulate a view.

I suggested a possible definition earlier. Unfortunately, this simple description begs further questions, including: What's meant by terms such as 'God,' 'Source,' or 'The Divine'? What's being referred to when we speak about what is 'sacred'? Can any universal definition be offered that satisfies the question—what does it mean to be 'spiritual'?

I suspect that there are no answers to such questions that will please everybody. All I will attempt to offer is limited to describing my understanding of these terms. This doesn't mean that these references are 'right,' but simply that they are better qualified than had I made no attempt to define them.

For me, something that is sacred is no more and no less than something that is related to, or an expression of, God. This includes objects and symbolism used in religious practices; buildings and spaces that are designated as places for worship, contemplation, and prayer; and scriptures, poems, and songs that inspire wonder and awe.

However, these things alone are too limited to encompass what I believe is fully sacred. For me, this description applies to every creature, every tree, every drop of an ocean, and every star in the sky. A sunrise or a rainbow declare the beauty of divine working in the world, as does the miracle of every child's birth, or the mystery of unconditional love that unites two people. Every person, every acre of land, and every breath is sacred–because we, and everything around us, are divine.

I'm not alone in having this view–followers of earth-based traditions, adherents of Shinto and Daoism, and indigenous peoples throughout history maintain the same.

My definition of divinity, or of 'God,' is simply 'The source of all life and supernatural intelligence that creates, destroys, and sustains everything that we experience, as well as much more that we do not see and can never comprehend.'

Because this power, essence, or being is far greater than anything we can ever conceive, acting beyond levels of consciousness and physical dimensions that are familiar to us, we can never adequately describe Who or What God is. The best that we can achieve is to appreciate something of the divine nature, Whoever we perceive Her, Him, It, or They to be.

Whether we see God as a person, as an invisible life force that is everywhere, as the roots of the trees and breath of the wind, or we go inside ourselves to sense a divine presence in our hearts, doesn't matter.

Whether we use the name 'Source,' 'Spirit,' 'Mother Earth,' 'Father Sky,' 'The One,' 'Everything That Is,' or one of a million or more other names, shouldn't be a concern to another person. In keeping with my definition of interfaith, the 'God of [your] understanding' should be described in whatever terms are most meaningful for you.

Defining what is meant by 'Spirit' is a little more problematic. This is difficult because it is a notion that evades normal consciousness and rational explanation. Spirit is intangible, easily confused with emotions and feelings, chemical and other bodily reactions, or ideas and sensations that might have their origin in the brain.

A spiritual sense is normally experienced arising from the heart or the gut, something that appears to have a voice and essence. It's a feeling that can lead to spontaneous, unexplained ecstasy and a welling-up of good feeling in the whole body, but which isn't obviously triggered by a physical, sensual experience.

For me, the 'spirit' is what exists at the very core of our being. It plays a vital role prompting our conscience, yet we are free to choose to ignore it. Even more mysterious, I and many others believe that our spirit is wholly merged with *The Spirit*—the primordial force that I refer to as divine. To be 'spiritual' is to connect with this, often in a way that might be regarded as mystical or supernatural. To be in touch with this spirit is nothing short of being in touch with God.

Of course, for those who need everything to be rationally explained or capable of being demonstrated scientifically, this is a concept that beggars belief. For the countless millions of us who believe we have enjoyed spiritual experiences, and who are ready to accept that there is much that remains hidden from a scientific lens, our belief in the unexplained might simply be referred to as 'faith.'

We have sketched out some basic ideas that might help us move forward to talking about 'interfaith initiatives,' or an 'interfaith movement.' But have we said enough? I suggest that we need to qualify how such things manifest further. This is something that we'll turn our attention to later.

We've already noted some of the more obvious possible ways of making sense of how interfaith manifests in human actions—the value of an appreciative dialogue between the followers and leaders of different faith traditions, recognizing the commonality in the central teaching of most faiths, and encouraging tolerance of peoples who hold different worldviews, among them.

These recognize the uniqueness of individual faith traditions and point to what might be ground for forming bridges between them. Any two or more organisations can arrive at a common statement of their response to issues that may be confronting the communities that they serve, or the world at large—assuming, of course, that there is a will to do so.

Offering platforms for representatives of faiths other than our own to speak at meetings, sharing in some form of worship, or simply fostering friendship between communities are some obvious ways on which the pillars of such a bridge might be built.

Such shared initiatives have gained popularity during recent years, although haven't always been without controversy. Still, these tend to be relatively isolated ventures, which often amount to little more than an agreement that "we must do this again next year". For me, serious interfaith dialogue needs to go much further, and what can be achieved under the interfaith label must extend far beyond occasional joint meetings and statements of solidarity on selected issues.

One further example of interfaith in action is to observe what happens when individuals who follow a particular faith path discover that their appreciation of what they believe can be informed by or enhanced through the teachings of other traditions.

This can apply to someone who describes themselves as being essentially (say) a Buddhist, but whose understanding of the teachings of their faith is given fresh meaning through their appreciation of what other traditions have to say about the same topic. Christians who bring mantra-based meditation into their daily spiritual practice are one example of those who've adopted a practice that has its roots in another faith [4].

Individuals who seek exposure to the worship styles, music, dance, spiritual practices, rituals, and scriptures of faiths other than their own may discover new ways of expressing their spiritual lives than might previously have been familiar to them. This doesn't mean that what they believe has fundamentally changed, but that they recognize that there may be far more ways for connecting with the sacred than they may have encountered within the practice of their tradition.

Those who don't subscribe to a particular faith tradition, but who recognize the common teachings of many faith paths might also fall into the category of interfaith practitioners. I believe that this group also includes those who wouldn't consider themselves to be religious and who don't attach to a faith tradition, but who nonetheless are open to the possibility of a greater power than they can conceive having a part to play in the evolving tapestry of life. Those who believe that the Earth is an organism with an intelligence might number among these [5].

If we take the view that interfaith may variously refer to forming bridges between institutions, with their well-contained statements of belief and rituals, and mixing aspects of what two or more traditions may have to offer, it's reasonable to ask how we might define what a faith tradition is in the first place.

Even to begin exploring what attaches to the name of a single religion is problematic. For a start, every religion is often represented by many different denominations–Roman Catholics, Protestants, Orthodox, so-called 'Non-conformist,' and more among Christians, for example; Mahayana, Theravada, and Vajrayana among Buddhists; Reform, Conservative, Orthodox and Reconstructionist among Jews, and so on.

Quite distinct differences in the beliefs, liturgies, and even texts may be adopted by different churches and other faith institutions of these diverse denominations.

In some cases, these distinctions have come about primarily by the styles of worship that appeal to different people–evangelical Christians preferring to freely allow the Spirit to express itself through dance and unconstrained movement, for example, while many Episcopalians find solace in contemplative practices.

In other cases, differences have resulted from alternative interpretations, sometimes marking out quite wide disparities in belief between the proponents of different sects or schools claiming to follow the same tradition.

Even within some individual faith communities, such differences can arise. At a church that I used to attend, for example, both traditional, liturgical 'high church' services and very informal, lively fellowship gatherings were offered, catering to the differing interests of its congregation.

Interfaith or multifaith?

I use the term 'interfaith' in this book, in preference to the also commonly used labels 'inter-religious' and 'multifaith.' For all practical purposes, at least in our discussion, either of these terms might be used interchangeably.

For me, 'interfaith' puts emphasis on the idea of individuals sharing their faiths, rather than attempting to align with or compromise their distinctive, organized or institutionalised religions. It's a term that has gained popularity during recent years, while 'inter-religious' has tended to be one that's preferred in academic circles.

We might usefully also consider the concepts of 'pluralism' and 'ecumenism.' The latter is taken to apply to the inter-workings of and sharing of a common purpose among Christian fellowships, although is occasionally used to describe initiatives which encourage a coming together of representatives of different faith traditions.

'Pluralism' is a label that's widely used in Christian circles to describe a viewpoint that there are many ways to find God, even though each person subscribes to a single tradition. From a pluralist's perspective, while the names and cultural references that are used to describe divinity may vary, the 'God' that is spoken about by different traditions is ultimately the same.

Pluralism is distinguished from 'inclusivism' and 'exclusivism.' Exclusivists have the most difficulty embracing an interfaith ethic, believing as they do that there is only one true path to salvation (or freedom from the bond of suffering that is a common lot of all people).

Furthermore, they hold that the only true path is the one that they follow. In their view, anyone that doesn't subscribe to their path follows a false creed. Exclusivists are to be found in every tradition.

By contrast, inclusivists accept that followers of traditions other than their own can enjoy a genuine religious experience and connect with The Divine, but they maintain that their path remains superior to those of others. Hence, some Tibetan traditions acknowledge that others' paths may lead them to enlightenment, but maintain that theirs is the preferable and most honourable route.

Inclusivist perspectives can be found among those who strive for interfaith tolerance and dialogue, but whose creed convinces them that theirs is the sole pure faith. Such a view is well illustrated by a recent statement of the Anglican Church, which represents a step toward tolerating the beliefs of non-Christians, but which doesn't shirk away from maintaining the crucial pillar of the belief that Christians subscribe to:

"We do assert that God can and does work in people of other religions, and indeed within other religions, and that this is by His Spirit. In the ultimate sense, salvation is defined by having Jesus Christ as its source and goal"[1].

What is a 'faith'?

Interfaith dialogue is only meaningful if we recognize what a faith or faith tradition is. This basic point is very clearly made by the academic Ataullah Siddiqui, in a reflection on the purpose of interfaith dialogue:

"There is no inter-faith without faith. A meaningful dialogue is only possible when people have a deep conviction that their faith has something to offer to the wider society in which they live"[2].

The distinctions marking out a faith might be summarised as one that:

- Has a clear creed, or statement of belief, that all members of the faith subscribe to,
- Holds regular gatherings, which tend to follow a familiar structure, and are overseen by one or more leaders or elders (although hierarchical structures and leadership influence might not always apply),
- Often has an adopted liturgy (a set form of worship), or performs rituals that are familiar to and meaningful for members of the faith community,

- Believes that there is one way for describing who or what 'The Divine' is, or alternatively, maintains that there is no personhood of God,
- Holds beliefs about the origins of the world, the purpose of life, the notion of human beings having a 'soul' or 'spirit,' and offers standardised teachings about life after death,
- Trusts one or more sacred texts as being divinely inspired,
- Requires fellow members to accept its teachings.

This list is by no means exhaustive, and may not fully apply to some more informal faith groups. However, it should help us characterise the general distinguishing marks of most denominations.

Each faith offers a perspective on the nature of life and death, and topics similar to those that we have just referred to. One or more historical characters may feature heavily in its teachings, and the text and fundamental beliefs that each of its denominations adopts typically evolved from a common beginning.

The same might, of course, be said of mythology, of Pagan and earth-based traditions, and the stories passed down like folklore. We perhaps shouldn't rush to distinguish these from what we might bracket under the label of 'faith.'

Indeed, what most people now commonly describe as Greek myths relate to a system of beliefs–a religion–that pervaded for many centuries; a faith tradition of old that may have relatively few adherents today may reveal truths and point to the nature of divinity and humanity no less than the impressions that can be drawn from the traditions that are popular today.

In general, though, our definition of a 'faith' appears to be something that's quite rigidly defined. To adopt a particular faith, a follower is expected to commit to its way of doing things, and to subscribe to a well-bounded set of beliefs.

However, this characterisation may be overly rigid for belief systems that don't fall under the category of a major faith tradition or institutionalised religion. Here, there is scope for varied and spontaneous acts of worship, with an intention for the direction of the group to be determined by the participatory membership, rather than the decision-making of a leader or leadership team.

The Quakers, for example, normally don't follow a rigid format at their gatherings. Silence allows for contemplation, with individuals only speaking when they feel led to do so. Such an approach allows the freedom for anyone to express whatever they feel inspired to bring to the group.

The Druid Order also embraces communal acts of worship and might be described as being an overarching philosophy that includes a variety of practices under its umbrella, rather than a single religion *per se*.

Some faith traditions go further, in openly embracing a broad base for their teaching. The Universalist Unitarian Church, for example, shuns dogma and strict creeds in favour of a faith that rests with each person's conscience.

While some Unitarians see themselves as 'liberal Christians,' Unitarianism embraces a wide variety of beliefs, including people who have Muslim, Jewish, Humanist, Buddhist, Pagan and Atheist perspectives. Its focus is to encourage a searching for truth from within, rather than from what is prescribed or taught from a pulpit. Some Quaker Societies similarly detach from a strict allegiance to Christian beliefs.

Bodies such as the Universalist Unitarian Church may be especially open to encouraging interfaith engagement in their teaching and activities, but where does this leave those denominations and institutions that we've characterised as being more dogmatic in what they teach?

The apparent insistence in many traditions that there is only one way would seem to preclude any possibility for a broad acceptance of any number of faiths providing a way to the truth, whatever level of agreement might exist regarding general principles for living, life purpose, and the ultimate nature of divinity.

Closer examination suggests that this need not be so. Islam, for example, recognizes Jews and Christians as 'peoples of The Book,' while most Hindus similarly have no difficulty accepting that other religions teach aspects of the truth.

Crucially, the fundamental teachings of the major faiths are far less contradictory than may at first glance be perceived. We'll examine the essential areas of overlap in the next chapter.

Happily, there are many who are willing to see that theirs is a tradition among many that offer ways to God. And even among those who maintain that theirs is the one true faith, large numbers still recognize the value of sharing a dialogue with others and having respect for their beliefs.

The great nineteenth century Harvard theologian Josiah Royce called this the mark of any true follower of God, observing that "nobody fully comprehends what religion is who imagines that his own religion is the only genuine religion"[3], and that, "the underlying motives of the higher religions are, after all, much more in agreement than the diversities of creeds and the apparent chaos of religious experiences would lead us to imagine"[4].

He didn't restrict his reference to religion as being solely meant for the traditional faiths either but saw that "Socrates and Plato and Sophocles are religious teachers from whom we have all directly or indirectly learned, whether we know it or not"[5].

This was also the view taken by the founder of The New Seminary for Interfaith Studies, which is still active in training ministers to serve people of all faiths. Rabbi Joseph Gelberman, with the support of other spiritual leaders, opened the school in New York in 1979, inspired by the view that a sharing of influence among religious communities would better serve humanity than by each operating alone.

Individuals who feel they can associate with a worldview such as Gelberman's may be able to achieve more by working together rather than in isolation, especially in bringing about community projects that aim to put into practise the virtues of compassion, standing firm against acts of violence committed in the name of religion, and in other areas that each holds dear to their purpose.

Is this all?

Dialogue. Tolerance. Appreciation of similarities. Finding illumination from the teachings of others. Working together in communities…We're beginning to build a strong list of reasons for faith communities to communicate and co-operate. But is this all that might be described under the interfaith name?

I believe that there is more.

Among those that I've met who describe themselves as belonging to an interfaith community are some of academic background, theologians, and others who've spent years in the clergy.

However, most are people who don't focus on the concerns of theology, but who strive to understand the basic tenets and principles for living and connecting with divinity. While some prefer a story to be presented in their language and culture, they nonetheless can find and appreciate the same teaching about (say) loving our neighbour, whether it's presented as a story from Buddhism, Sikhism, Islam, or Navajo wisdom.

It's in the focus of interfaith ministry where I believe we can find the strongest guidance to what interfaith is about. Certainly, this advocates dialogue and gaining understanding and learning from different traditions, even integrating the odd spiritual practice or two into our own. However, it's primarily about helping people to connect with their inner selves and divinity at the place where they are, including those who are agnostic or describe themselves as lacking any religious belief. It's a mindset that embraces those who prefer to seek to understand in mythology, the esoteric writings of nineteenth century philosophers, or New Age teachings.

For me, the key notions at the nub of interfaith are then: 'helping to connect,' and 'connecting with.' The first concerns meeting others where they are; the second relates to offering ourselves with an open heart from the place where we are.

Recognizing that while we may not be coming from the same place, we seek the same truth, reach for the same destination, and through the same spirit, can unite in celebrating and embracing the same 'God' (albeit, we may perceive of Him, Her, They, or It in many different ways).

This is more than finding common ground; it's an experience through which we become one people, connected through the heart rather than through ideology.

For partakers in the interfaith ethos, the terms 'God,' 'Source,' 'The Universe' or any other label for divinity then become 'The God of your Understanding,' and 'faith' translates as 'believing in something greater than is apparent to our rational minds.' This is a perspective that respects all traditions, believing that none presents an exclusive path to becoming fully human, and–ultimately–to being connected with everything that's divine.

The need for intra-faith understanding

A readiness to tolerate and deeply respect the worldviews of others must also apply within a single faith tradition. Christian evangelicals and mystics do well when they recognize where each of their different souls is at, respect each other, and see that they may themselves change. This contrasts with a mindset that wants to polarise positions or try to 'force' a conversion. The need for improved intra-faith tolerance in the world today may indeed be as strongly required as for respect between faiths.

We might all find a way toward better-appreciating others by learning to dwell more in the heart than in our headspace. As one variation of the Buddhist Metta lovingkindness prayer puts it, "May all beings know their wholeness, may all beings dwell in the heart" [6]

Clive Johnson

CHAPTER 3

Where is the common ground?

THERE ARE THOUGHT TO BE more than 6,000 religions in the world[1]. To explore the differences and commonality between these would be something of a tall order, to say the least, especially since perspectives relating to such concepts as 'the self' vary enormously between traditions.

Furthermore, differences exist within single faith traditions as they are presented in different geographies, and at varying times in history. A study of Buddhism in Vietnam would most likely yield a different analysis from an exploration of Buddhist practice in Nepal, for example; the Christianity that prevailed in Asia for close to 1,000 years after the earthly lifetime of Jesus might be very different from that, say, practised by Greek Orthodox Christians in the current century.

Despite these differences, the academic discipline of comparative religion does attempt to make sense of the differences and similarities between faiths, with a view to enhancing understanding of the different ethical and ideological approaches that underpin the belief systems of the world's peoples. Its work has achieved much in illuminating what unites and what sets apart today's major faiths.

Inevitably, this is a discipline that needs to acknowledge other fields of study, such as anthropological and sociological perspectives. Malory Nye, a professor of multiculturalism at the Al-Maktoum Institute in Scotland, points out that comparative religion isn't an attempt to reach a consensus view on the fundamental truths that may underlie every faith tradition. In his book 'Religion: The Basics,' he observes:

"What the study of religion and culture is not about, is finding 'ultimate' truths or answers. Liberation, salvation, morality, belief, and many other such key concepts may be subject matter under examination when studying religion, but we can speculate *ad infinitum* as to which set of ideas is closer to the 'truth.'"[2]

Given such a position, can any common ground be found between the different faiths? Can there be any reasonable basis for an interfaith dialogue that seeks to emphasise areas of agreement, or for the position that we've taken, that all (or at least most) faith traditions teach similar things, and insist upon their members following similar moral codes, even if these teachings are couched in many different ways?

Happily, as we'll see, there are many commonalities, and this common ground tends to address matters of fundamental importance for each faith. Happily too, the leaders of different traditions speak about much that they can agree upon and be partners in advocating.

Without attempting the impossible task of reviewing all of these commonalities, it may be helpful for us to summarise some of the common ground here.

Recognizing this should give us hope that there is scope for followers of different faiths to not only engage in a dialogue but also to enjoy the experience of worshipping and sharing fellowship with each other.

The golden and silver rules

Most pertinent of the fundamental injunctions to be found in the holy writings of many cultures are the so-called 'golden' and 'silver rules.'

A popular rendering of the golden rule is 'Do unto others as you would have them do unto you.' Its complement, the silver rule, puts the focus on not harming others, instructing, 'Do nothing to others you would not have done to you.'

The golden and silver rules are unambiguously stated in many scriptures, for example:

"None of you has faith until he loves for the people what he loves for himself; and until he loves a person only for the sake of Allah the Exalted" (Islam, Musnad Ahmad, Number 13463, Sahih).

"Do to others as you would have them do to you" (Christian, Luke 6:31, NIV).

"Hurt not others with that which pains yourself" (Buddhist, Udanavarga 5:18).

"No one is my enemy, none a stranger and everyone is my friend" (Sikh, Guru Arjan Dev).

"This is the sum of duty: do not do to others what would cause pain if done to you" (Hindu, Mahabharata 5:1517).

"Be charitable to all beings, love is the representative of God" (Shinto, Ko-ji-ki Hachiman Kasuga).

"The sage has no interest of his own but takes the interests of the people as his own. He is kind to the kind; he is also kind to the unkind: for Virtue is kind. He is faithful to the faithful; he is also faithful to the unfaithful: for Virtue is faithful" (Taoist, Tao Te Ching, Ch. 49).

"And it harms no one, do what thou wilt" ("Do what ever you will, as long as it harms nobody, including yourself") (Celtic/Wiccan, The Wiccan Rede).

"Blessed is he who preferreth his brother before himself" (Bahá, Bahá'u'lláh).

"One going to take a pointed stick to pinch a baby bird should first try it on himself to feel how it hurts" (Yoruba People, Nigeria).

"A man should wander about treating all creatures as he himself would be treated" (Jain, Sutrakritanga 1.11.33).

"You shall love your neighbour as yourself" (Judaism, Leviticus 19:18).

"Whatever is disagreeable to yourself do not do unto others" (Zoroastrianism, Shayast-na-Shayast 13:29).

Both rules are also widely accepted as a basis for ethical living outside of religious contexts. Philosophers, law makers, and sociologists are among their advocates.

Humanists proclaim "Don't do things you wouldn't want to have done to you"[3].

Confucius, in common with other Chinese sages, made it a centrepiece in his teaching, declaring, "Do not unto another that you would not have him do unto you. Thou needest this law alone. It is the foundation of all the rest" (Confucius, *Analects* 15:23).

The Greek philosophers, whose words have influenced so much of Western thinking, were similarly forthcoming in adding their voice. For example:

"We should conduct ourselves toward others as we would have them act toward us" (Aristotle, 384 BCE).

"Do not to your neighbour what you would take ill from him" (Pittacus, 650 BCE).

"Act toward others as you desire them to act toward you" (Isocrates, 338 BCE).

We could easily go on.

Having love and respect for others are part and parcel of following the rules, and these, in turn, must also be directed to The Divine. In keeping the rules, we cannot but help to follow the First Commandment that was given to both the Hebrews and the Christians, to "love the Lord your God with all your heart, soul, and strength" (*Deuteronomy* 6:5, *Matthew* 22:37).

Indeed, perhaps the rules aren't so much about acting, as thinking. They don't require us to be perfect or to turn the other cheek. Rather, as one writer puts it, "[They] alert us to everyday self-absorption, and the failure to consider our impacts on others. They remind us that we are peers to others who deserve comparable consideration. They suggest a general orientation toward others, an outlook for seeing our relations with them. At the least, we should not impact others negatively, treating their interests as secondary"[4].

Self-absorption may be the ultimate sin (to use Judeo-Christian terminology), not only because it distracts us from honouring the interests of others, but because by so doing, it stops us from staying in touch with The Divine. If God is within everyone and everything, the moment we deliberately ignore or forget this is the moment we lose touch with Him.

Taking a faith perspective, to be godless is to be separated from the purpose for being. Without being connected to The Divine, loving and participating in Her gift of life, is to be doomed to an existence that will never bring fulfilment. Worse, it's an existence that is 'unsaved,' or unable to overcome the eternal cycle of birth, death, and rebirth that brings suffering and a hopeless quest for satisfaction and security.

This notion of separation from divinity and the suffering that results from it is described in very different ways in the scriptures of different faiths. However, whether we speak of escaping the wheel of *samsāra* to realize *nirvana*, to follow the Buddhists' portrayal, or prefer images of the torturing of hell, as depicted by the Abrahamic faiths, the separation is the same.

In each case, we need 'saving,' and this cannot be achieved by our own efforts alone. However, when we "pray continually" (*1 Thessalonians* 5:17) or "remember Allah much" (*Qur'an* 33:21), we come back into contact with God.

It might be concluded from the preceding discussion that several of the principles of faith teachings are fully wrapped up with the golden and silver rules. Love, respect, honouring The Divine before all else, recognizing our need to be saved, and seeing that the means of salvation lies outside putting ourselves first...these are among the major themes in teachings of most traditions, and they are all intimately related.

Major themes in common teachings

Much religious teaching focuses on these very themes. There is little disagreement on the concerns that matter.

Let's spend a moment to take stock of this simple, but often overlooked fact. A few reflections on comparative scriptures might help us to focus on the common, essential teachings, although these could easily be added to many times over.

God is One

There is one God, and this God (Source, Essence, Nature, Being, All-pervading Life, The Absolute, etc.) is the same, however She, He, They or It is described.

> *"To you it was shown, that you might know that the Lord Himself is God; there is none other besides Him" (Deuteronomy 4:35, NKJV).*

> *"Say: He, Allah, is The One.*

> *Allah, the independently absolute, The eternal.*

> *He begets not, nor was He begotten.*

> *And, there is none like Him" (Qur'an, Surah 112).*

> *"There is only One God" (Chief Seattle).*

God is omnipresent

God is everywhere, filling heaven and the earth (Jeremiah 23:24), is diffused in the ten directions, in all the earth and sky (*Sri Guru Granth Sahib*).

> *"All this [Universe] is verily Brahman"* (*Chandogya Upanishad, 3.14.1*).

> *"To Allah belongs the East and the West; wherever you turn, this is Allah's face. Allah is All-Encompassing (Omnipresent) and All-Knowing"* (*Qur'an, 2:115*).

God dwells within us

God dwells in our hearts (*Baghavad-Gita* 10:11), being with us where we are (*Qur'an*, 57:4), the Kingdom of God is in our midst (*Luke* 17:21).

> *"Man is My mystery and I am his mystery, for I am he himself and he is also I Myself"* (*The Prophet Muhammad, Hadith Qudsi*).

> *"The yogi learns to find God in the cave of his heart. Whenever he goes, he carries with him the blissful consciousness of God's Presence"* (*Paramahansa Yogananda*[5]).

> *"Forget self and identify Ahura Mazda in every being and in everything"* (*Zoroaster*) [7].

> *"Even as the scent dwells within the flower, so God within thine own heart forever abides"* (*Guru Nanak*).

> *"The first peace, which is most important, is that which comes within the souls of men when they*

realize their relationship, their oneness, with the universe and all its powers, and when they realize that at the center of the universe dwells Wakan-Tanka, and that this center is really everywhere, it is within each of us" (Native American).

Going into the depths of religious teachings, we can learn that God is nearer to us than we can ever imagine. Jesus tells us that the kingdom of God reigns within each one of us. The *Bhagavad Gita* says that God dwells in everything. The Upanishads reveal that God is hidden in all living beings. The message could not be clearer.

A person who knows himself knows God

When we discover our true self, we come to understand that we are divine and that God works through us and experiences Her Universe through us.

"Whosoever knows himself knows his Lord" (Hadith of Rasul (SAW)).

"He who knows himself is enlightened" (Tao Te Ching, Ch. 33).

"Who knoweth Him, knoweth himself and is not afraid to die" (Atharva-Veda, 10.8.44).

"He who knows what God is, and who knows what man is, has attained. Knowing what God is, he knows that he himself proceeded therefrom" (Chuang-tse, Ch. 6).

"The seeker is he who is in search of himself" (Sri Nisargadatta Maharaj[6]).

Spiritual knowledge can be found by anyone

If we are earnest about seeking God, we will discover God. Spiritual consciousness may be a hidden treasure, but if we make a genuine effort to inquire into what is true, all faith traditions teach that we will receive insight.

> "I am easy of access to that ever steadfast yogi who, O Partha, constantly meditates on Me and gives no thought to anything else" (Baghavad-Gita 8:14).

> "All who dwell on earth may find you" (Jewish[7]).

> "Ask, and it shall be given you; seek, and ye shall find; knock, and it shall be opened unto you" (Matthew 7:7).

> "Everyone can be a yogi, right where he is now" (Paramahansa Yogananda[8]).

God is The Great I AM, The universal name of God

God may be addressed by many names, but all ascribe the common meaning, "I AM." Sri Nisargadatta Maharaj explains the "I AM" as "an abstraction in the mind of the Stateless State, of the Absolute, or the Supreme Reality, called Parabrahman: it is pure awareness, prior to thoughts, free from perceptions, associations, memories"[9].

> "I am the Self, O Gudekesa, seated in the hearts of all creatures. I am the beginning, the middle, and the end of all beings'"(Baghavad-Gita Ch. 10).

> "I AM that I AM" (Exodus 3:14).

> "'I am,' thrice exclaimed The Bab, 'I am, I am, the promised One! I am the One Whose name you have for a thousand years invoked, at Whose mention you have risen, whose advent you have longed to witness, and the hour of Whose revelation you have prayed God to hasten'"[10].

All of humanity is united when we are at one with God

If every person is divine, then everyone is united by the same Source. We are all, so to speak, each other's brothers and sisters, or offspring of God. This sense of unity is made perfect when we fully merge into the essence of God, letting our egoistic selves slip away.

> "Man himself is the image and offspring of the kami" (Shinto[11]).

> "The man whose self is disciplined in yoga, whose perception is the same everywhere, sees himself in all creatures, and all creatures in himself" (Bhagavad-Gita 6:29).

> "One thing we know. All men are brothers" (Chief Seattle).

> "To think of God is to lose yourself in Him. The mind disappears and God only is" (Swami Ramdas).

> "All creatures are members of the one family of God" (Saying of the Prophet Muhammad).

> "There is no Gentile or Jew, circumcised or uncircumcised, Barbarian, Scythian, slave or free, but Christ is all, and is in all" (Colossians 3:11).

> "All people are your children, whatever their belief, whatever their shade of skin" (Jewish Prayer Book).

Man does not live by bread alone; we are spiritual beings

Life affords much deeper blessings than those that can be appreciated by the senses alone. People have an inner life; we each have a soul [8].

> "And no soul can die but with Allah's permission" (Qur'an 3:145).

> "For the soul there is never birth nor death. It is not slain when the body is slain" (Bhagavad-Gita 2:20).

> "Store up for yourselves treasures in heaven, where neither moth nor rust destroys, and where thieves do not break in or steal" (Matthew 6:20).

> "Seek spiritual riches within. What you are is much greater than anyone or anything else you have ever yearned for" (Paramahansa Yogananda).

> "Be [not] afraid of those killing the body but not being able to kill the soul" (Matthew 10:28).

We should give up hoping in the self and worldly things

Our first task is to "Stand up for God," and "let the world go" (Swami Vivekananda). It is only when our mind stops being distracted by the false attractions of the material world and worldly measures of success that it "becomes free, radiant and joyful; at death, one is no longer subject to rebirth. Nirvana is the ultimate happiness"[12].

> "Surrender the grasping disposition of your selfishness, and you will attain to that sinless calm state of mind which conveys perfect peace, goodness, and wisdom"[13].

> "He who gives himself up to His supreme will, wins the goal. No other action counts in achieving this end" (Guru Nanak).

> "Whosoever desires the life of the world and its glitter; to them We shall pay in full [the wages of] their deeds therein, and they will have no diminution therein. They are those for whom there is nothing in the hereafter but Fire; and vain are the deeds they did therein" (Qur'an 11: 15-16).

We are to love God first

If we fully and constantly love God, we will become at one with Him, and so be free from earthly suffering.

> "That which is most needed is a loving heart"[14].

> "Unalloyed love of God is the essential thing. All else is unreal" (Sri Ramakrishna[15]).

"You shall love the Lord your God with all your heart, and with all your soul, and with all your mind. This is the great and first commandment" (Matthew 22:37, Deuteronomy 6:4).

"Help us to walk the sacred path of life without difficulty, with our minds and hearts continually fixed on You!" (Native American, Wakan-Tanka[16]).

We will reap what we sow

Karma is a natural law, whether we recognize it or not. Every one of our thoughts, intentions, and actions has a consequence.

"Whatsoever a man soweth, that shall he also reap. For he that soweth to his flesh shall of the flesh reap corruption; but he that soweth to the Spirit shall of the Spirit reap life everlasting" (Galatians 6: 7-8, KJV).

"You have planted wickedness, you have reaped evil, you have eaten the fruit of deception" (Hosea 10:13, NIV).

"They shall reap the fruit of what they did, and you of what you do! Of their merits there is no question in your case!" (Qur'an, 2:141).

"One day you will have to reap what you have sown...If you sow a thorn you will reap a thorn" (ZOROASTER[17]).

"And as is his desire, so is his will; and as is his will, so is his deed; and whatever deed he does, that he will reap" (Brihadaranyaka-Upanishad Part 3).

> *"For naught is reaped save that which hath been sown, and naught is taken up save that which hath been laid down, unless it be through the grace and bestowal of the Lord" (Bahá'í, Baha'u'llah[18]).*

> *"When he is doing evil, the fool does not realize it. The idiot is punished by his own deeds, like one is scorched by fire" (Buddhist[19]).*

> *"What you give you get, ten times over" (Yoruba[20]).*

We need to repent

Repentance can feel like a very heavily loaded concept, involving great regret and a desire to atone for our failings. However, we might more helpfully consider it as being a change of mind–one that is directed to being at one with The Divine, once we recognize that we have separated ourselves from Her.

For Hindus, to practice *prayashchit* is to deeply regret past actions, but also to resolve to start afresh. Buddhists who recognize that their lack of compassion and wrong actions don't originate from *Pure Consciousness* determine to break from their attachments, aversions, and delusions. For Christians, the action of *metanoia* is a changing of heart, a commitment to setting their mind on modelling the behaviour and teachings of Jesus.

> "For all the evil deeds I have done in the past,
> Created by my body, speech and mind,

From beginningless greed, hatred and delusion,
I now know shame and repent them all."
(Buddhist[21]).

> "More and more the heart is filled with remorse against misdeeds conducted, more and more the body gets purified of the misdeed. And hence by cleaning the heart one gets rid of sin" (Manu Smriti 11.229) [9].

> "This is what the Sovereign LORD, the Holy One of Israel, says: 'In repentance and rest is your salvation, in quietness and trust is your strength'" (Isaiah 30:15).

> "Repent, then, and turn to God, so that your sins may be wiped out, that times of refreshing may come from the Lord" (Acts 3:19).

We need to forgive and know that God forgives us when we repent

To fail to forgive means that we are forever locked in a past state; either we or those we need to forgive, cannot move forward without feeling alienated from the one we (or they) have let down.

> "The most beautiful thing a man can do is to forgive wrong" (Jewish[22]).

> "If Allah were to punish Men for their wrongdoing, He would not leave, on the (Earth), a single living creature," "And seek forgiveness of Allah . Indeed, Allah is Forgiving and Merciful" (Qur'an 16:61; Qur'an 73:20).

> "By three things the wise person may be known. What three? He sees a shortcoming as it is. When

he sees it, he tries to correct it. And when another acknowledges a shortcoming, the wise one forgives it as he should" (teaching of The Buddha[23]).

"And when you stand praying, if you hold anything against anyone, forgive them, so that your Father in heaven may forgive you your sins" (Mark 11:25).

Wow! Here we can plainly see that there's quite a lot that different faith traditions share in common, if only most of us might more readily recognize this!

In my reading, these are essentially the teachings that matter in the 'big six,' as well as for most other traditions. Most of the many million other holy writings and sayings are expositions on these, or codified practices for believers to abide by that flow from them.

However, even in their codifying of rules to live by, most traditions advocate similar moral precepts, if tempered by local culture and situation. The injunctions not to lie, steal, and commit murder are universal. The Ten Commandments, the Ten Precepts of the Buddha, and the *Bhagavad-Gita* (chapter 16) are unanimous in their promotion of non-violence, non-judgement, and showing compassion to others.

To be peaceable means that we recognize all others as being unseparated from or foreign to ourselves–"since all men are the offspring of kami," declares the Way of Shinto, then "each individual is worthy of proper respect"[24]. The Buddha said that showing goodwill toward all beings is the "true religion"; and if we make peace, the gospel writer recounts, we will become "known as the Children of God" (*Matthew* 5:9).

This need to strive for peace seems to be a core aim of at least one gathering of religious leaders and scholars, who came together in Monterrey, Mexico, in September 2007. This major conference highlighted several common areas of concern shared by the fifteen faiths represented[25]:

- Materialism and spiritual decline, a concern that consumer behaviour is leading to an erosion in individuals' spiritual lives.
- Profaning the Earth, a concern with threats to the environment and the destruction of the natural world that is held by most faith traditions to be sacred.
- Domination and exploitation, a perceived threat to spiritual values from powerful self-interested nations and corporations; for example, as expressed through the subjugation of peoples to standards comparable with slav-

ery in the interests of supplying rich nations with cheap goods.
- Radicalism, a concern that some traditions are being hijacked by radical followers, including incitement toward intolerance and violence. If unopposed, such radicalism threatens the very identity of these religions and can encourage widespread distrust for peoples of faith.

Common to these concerns are cries for justice, respect for the sacred, and equal treatment among peoples. Such are fundamental tenets of each of the traditions that contributed to this debate, and which are so clearly in keeping with the golden and silver rules.

What about the differences? The problem with particularity

Of course, there are many differences of dogma and practice among religions, not to mention teachings that appear to be at odds. However, it seems to me that these are often due to differences in understanding or interpretation.

One obvious point of departure here is those who see that the deities of other believers aren't the true God (and the scriptures are clear that there is no deity except for the true God).

This perspective becomes divisive when individuals cannot see that the God of others is the same as their God, even though the stories, names, occasion-

Understanding Interfaith

ally multiple manifestations and avatars, and ways of worshipping and depicting this God are as varied as can be imagined.

To worship an idol is to honour something that doesn't demonstrate the teachings mentioned above. An idol isn't simply something that is different to my or your way of picturing God (not that it's ever possible to have a complete picture of God, as I explore in my anthology, *Picturing God*); it's something completely different altogether

Muslims and Christians may disagree over whether or not the Godhead is a Trinity, and fundamentally (for Christians) over whether Jesus died as a sacrifice for our sins. Muslim and Christian views may conflict with Buddhists over whether there can ever be an escape from hell for those whose deeds or lack of faith have condemned them there. And followers of Hinduism pray to many deities.

Theologians and religious teachers will each have their views on such differences, and many will argue that these cannot be squared. My view is that whether one believes that there can be a coming together of understanding on such points often depends on how the teaching of each tradition is interpreted.

If we take the perspective that we can only escape the continuous trauma of life, death, and rebirth by being fully reunited with God, and that The Divine exists outside of time as we comprehend it, then it seems to me possible to reconcile an idea of being permanently stuck in hell with the Buddhist idea of escaping *samsara*.

As for the Christian notion of the Trinity, and Hindu and others' attention to many different deities, might these not be very human ways of coping with a God Who manifests in many different ways, or be alternative expressions of What or Who is the one and same God?

If God is in everything and is perfected in the individuals who surrender fully to Him, then Jesus is the perfect expression of God in human form—an avatar or incarnation, in the same way as are Buddha and Krishna. God's Spirit breathes through us, but this is still God.

Similarly, all the avatars, gods, goddesses and their consorts in the polytheistic faiths are really different manifestations, apparitions, or expressions of the one same God—for Hindus, there is only *one* Brahman.

The question of particularity, or concerning the need to acknowledge Jesus's sacrifice as the means for salvation, is less easy to resolve with non-Christian viewpoints. Much depends here on how the Passion of Christ is interpreted, and indeed, on whether we place our focus on the historical Jesus when talking about 'Christ' ('The anointed one').

For me, many mysteries remain attached to the crucifixion that I don't fully understand. I believe that Jesus's sacrifice and glorious rebirth is meant to point us to our own need to surrender our allegiance

Understanding Interfaith

to the ways of the world and become fully reunited with God.

By giving up that which separates us from God and turning our mind to stop thinking and acting in ways that have caused this separation in our lives before, we become reunited with Him, and without condition or penalty (in other words, we are forgiven). To my mind, this is no different than what is written in The *Qur'an*, that "The right course has become clear from the wrong" (*Qur'an* 2.256).

Translations of texts can themselves open up a risk of misinterpretation when reading or hearing a holy text in our mother tongue. The Sufi scholar and linguist Neil Douglas-Klotz, for example, offers alternative renderings for the Aramaic sayings of Jesus. Thus in his rendering, the familiar transliteration of the Lord's Prayer, "Our Father, Who art in heaven, hallowed be Thy Name," becomes "Oh Thou, from Whom the breath of life comes, Who fills all realms of sound, light, and vibration. May Your light be experienced in my utmost holiest," among many other reinterpretations offered by him[26].

However, there remain many who say that the inspired word of God survives any translation, and that scripture is always the 'living Word.' We cannot easily square these perspectives with those of Douglas-Klotz and others.

Moreover, since spiritual insight invariably flows from a mystical experience and attuning of the heart, those who rely on the intellectual argument for understanding scripture may not be able to understand that which cannot always easily be expressed in words or ways that might satisfy a rational mind.

With this in mind, we might do well to take note of the Hindu wisdom to "Follow the Spirit of the Scriptures, not the words–study the words, no doubt, but look behind them to the thought they indicate; And having found it, throw the words away, as chaff when you have sifted out the grain"[27].

If the ultimate truth is to recognize that The Divine lives within us and that all else we hold to have value is illusory and false, then we might find commonality and solace in any one of the holy texts that we are most familiar with.

If being born in any part of the world, at any time in history, and to any parentage affords the same opportunity to discover this truth, then we might conclude that no one faith is superior to another. Where the truth is taught and comprehended, this is all that ultimately matters.

CHAPTER 4

How are interfaith perspectives being expressed?

AS MUCH AS THERE is considerable common ground between faiths, there appears to have been a growing awareness and acknowledgement of this commonality during recent years. We may well be, in the words of Wayne Teasdale, at the beginning of an "inter-spiritual age"[1].

This isn't a particularly new phenomenon—in Christianity, the early Church Fathers were very enthusiastic about the teachings of Judaism, Greek philosophy, and Indian sages. This had followed an 'Axial Age' of belief, which prevailed in several regions of the world in the millennium before the time of

Jesus. In a wide-ranging book, the eminent historian Karen Armstrong reveals the common concerns of this period that linked the teaching of such luminaries as Buddha, Socrates, Confucius, and Jeremiah[2].

Drawing on painstaking research, she concludes that "...all the traditions that were developed during the Axial Age pushed forward the frontiers of human consciousness and discovered a transcendent dimension...it is not what you believe but how you act that leads to enlightenment"[3].

What is new today is the level of contact between peoples of different cultural and religious backgrounds, made possible by the easy movement of individuals and mass communications that have become available in the modern age.

A coming together of cultures within single societies has helped foster close relations between groups of people who formally regarded each other as 'the other.' This, in turn, has prompted an increasing appreciation of the perspectives of others, and among growing populations.

These relationships have moved beyond mere dialogue, curiosity in, and an openness to consider the similarity of what others have to say. Rather, in the words of the Jewish philosopher Martin Buber, "When they move beyond themselves to discover the other person as an equal, [a person] discovers a basic reality, a 'sphere between,' that links humanity in some greater wholeness"[4].

In other words, a close encounter with a tradition other than one's own very often yields an authentic religious experience, gives new perspective and insight into aspects of what is taught by one's own faith, and brings about an awareness that the spiritual experience of another may not be very different from one's own.

Excepting encounters with others' worldviews that have come about as a result of personal relationships, mass travel, and social media, many opportunities have arisen for (for example) Western spiritual seekers to become exposed to Eastern ideologies. The popularity of yoga, transcendental meditation, and *ayurveda* healing practices are among examples of imported disciplines that have gained widespread popularity in Western society during recent decades.

At the same time, in the secular world, scientists, politicians, lobby groups, and others have bought pressure to bear on national governments to cooperate in facing up to what are generally acknowledged as being universal problems that require a global response–the awesome challenges we are facing as a result of climate change, exploiting the Earth's natural resources, and changing demography, among them.

During the twentieth century, two devastating and prolonged world wars prompted the setting up of organisations whose primary purpose was to foster world peace–firstly, in the form of the League of Nations, and latterly, with the United Nations. In Europe, the EU– or rather its predecessor, the EEC–was also initially created with this same intention in mind.

Such organisations have recognized the importance of interfaith dialogue and cooperation. The United Nations not only upholds the rights of any person of any religion in its universal Universal Declaration of Human Rights (1948), but in 1981, its General Assembly adopted a resolution that "Freedom of religion and belief should also contribute to the attainments of the goals of world peace, social justice, and friendship among peoples"[5].

Faith-based initiatives that lobby for action to face up to the world's major problems, or which direct relief for humanitarian crises, inevitably share common ground, irrespective of the tradition from which they originated.

It's fair to say that a truly global initiative to foster strong relationships, understanding, and sharing of experiences among religious faiths predates the twentieth century. The World's Parliament of Religions, an organisation dedicated to "promot[ing] inter-religious harmony" (www.parliamentofreligions.org), held its inaugural meeting in Chicago in 1893. Albeit, its first gathering was led by a conviction by its initiators that the representatives of all faiths attending would "perfect [their] wisdom through Jesus Christ"[6].

One century later, the renamed Parliament of the World's Religions, showed signs of being a truly harmonious and egalitarian movement. One commentator, Imam and author Abdul Malik Mujahid, describes it as essentially being "a big conversation"[7].

An extensive consultation document by Professor Hans Küng, published in the 1990s, 'Toward a Global Ethic: An Initial Declaration,' declared a shared commitment to non-violence, justice, tolerance, truth-telling, and human rights. More than 200 representatives from forty separate faith traditions added their signatures to the declaration. Today, the parliament convenes every five years in a different city and is active in a wide range of activities.

One extensive study of fifteen faith traditions for the parliament[8] documents hundreds of initiatives that have been launched in the interest of fostering interfaith dialogue and community.

However, the picture of interfaith activity that emerges from this report by no means acknowledges universal acceptance of an interfaith mindset around the world. Interfaith activity is revealed to be most developed in the UK, Canada, and the USA.

The report notes that interfaith centres have grown up in major cities in Latin America and Europe, although local programs are less in evidence outside of areas showing a marked mix of religious affiliations among their populations. Increasing, though still restricted, religious tolerance in Russia and other former Soviet states has led to the beginnings of an interfaith dialogue, including the foundation of the Interreligious Council of Russia and similar councils in some other countries.

In Asia, an on-going dialogue among some religious groups, local and national councils, and a large interfaith organization in India have been prompted by a desire to forge bilateral dialogues (such as between Buddhists and Muslims). Indonesia shows a particularly high level of interfaith activity, while in Japan and South Korea, the survey notes the strong involvement of new religious movements in interfaith participation.

Faith groups that are in the minority, for example, Christians in northern India, have also often been active in pursuing conversations and co-operation with others.

An interfaith movement in Australia is emerging, while in South Africa, a historic Inter-Faith Peace Summit was held in 2002, involving representatives from across Africa. Regional conferences have also taken place, and interfaith groups have been active in response to civil wars and conflicts that continue to unsettle the continent (for example, the Inter-Faith Mediation Center in Nigeria, the Interreligious Council of Sierra Leone, and the Sudan Inter-Religious Council; all founded since the 1990s).

Groups devoted to coexistence have been formed in parts of the Middle East, although inter-religious tolerance continues to threaten the prospects for a lasting peace in the region (most recently, this has been compounded by the rise of ISIS and years of civil war and instability in Syria and Iraq). Several states in the region, as well as in North Africa and elsewhere, continue to deny freedom of expression to their citizens.

Despite this varied picture of geographical initiatives presented, the report does shine a spotlight on the wide range of "organizations, camps, television shows, books, press releases, photography exhibits, youth and adult educational curricula, trips, declarations, conferences, newsletters, regular dinners, fellowships, lectures, blogs, websites, manufacturers, ethical investment funds, sporting events, academic programs, awards, gardens, film viewings, and media-watchdog groups" that are contributing to this movement[9].

Examples of partnering initiatives between different faith communities abound. Some case studies cited by the report demonstrate the diversity of initiatives undertaken in different parts of the world. For example:

> The Singapore Baha'i Centre hosted an event for young people of all faiths to create a million paper lotuses as a symbol of goodwill and harmony.
>
> The World Council of Muslims for Interfaith Relations (WCMIR), based in New York, aims to foster mutual understanding and friendly relations among the people of different faiths through education and an interactive forum.
>
> The Doha International Center for Interfaith Dialogue, founded in 2007, aims to spread a "culture of dialogue, the peaceful coexistence of humanity and the acceptance of others."

The Children of Abraham hosts an on-line community for Jewish and Muslim students to interact with each other as one group.

Open Doors, Open Minds is an adult education program bringing Jews and Christians together.

The National Aboriginal and Torres Strait Islander Ecumenical Commission (NATSIEC), together with the National Council of Churches in Australia (NCCA), works for a fair deal for Aboriginal and Torres Strait Islander Australians, and for the healing of the Australian nation.

The Iberic Pagan Union is a nationwide association in Spain that encourages its members to participate in various programs offered by other religious traditions, notably in Catalonia, where the Friends of UNESCO are working for interreligious dialogue.

Gobind Sadan is an international interfaith community for all people and a place of pilgrimage with centres in India and the U.S.

The Three Faiths Forum, headquartered in London, fosters friendship, goodwill, and understanding among people of the three Abrahamic faiths.

The Jambudvipa Trust, based in Pune, India, hosts conferences and workshops to help people from different castes and faith backgrounds come together and transcend their differences.

> The Federation of Jain Associations in North America (JAINA) works to encourage an exchange of views among the other major religions of the world, with the intention of promoting harmony, trust and peace.

As these examples show, retreat centres, interfaith conferences, and national and international councils have been set up with the express intention of bringing peoples of different faiths together.

Significant, often ambitious, interfaith initiatives have continued to take root since the parliament's 2008 Survey.

For example, a world interfaith week, first proposed to the United Nations General Assembly by King Abdullah II bin Al-Hussein of Jordan in 2010 and now celebrated as The World Interfaith Harmony Week, has captured the imagination of many.

In unanimously approving the resolution to establish this annual celebration, the UN affirmed "that mutual understanding and inter-religious dialogue constitute important dimensions of a culture of peace", and "Encourages all States to support, on a voluntary basis, the spread of the message of interfaith harmony and goodwill in the world's Churches, Mosques, Synagogues, Temples and other places of Worship during that week based on Love of God and Love of the Neighbour, or based on Love of the Good and Love of the Neighbour, each according to their own religious traditions or convictions"[10].

The notion for a week of interfaith activities and inter-community sharing achieved further traction in the UK, with the 2008 publication by the UK Government of 'Face to Face and Side by Side–a Framework for Partnership in our Multi-Faith Society.' Prompted by this strategy for bringing communities together, the Inter Faith Network for the UK proposed an annual Inter-Faith Week, which has achieved considerable success since its first launch in 2009.

Events organized as a part of the week may be as simple as a communal service. Speaking to attendees of one such event a couple of years ago, a service involving worship led by representatives of different faiths at a church in Brighton&Hove, UK, I was struck by how many people found the experience to be uplifting. "I loved the imam's call to prayer," commented one among the congregation; "This was so beautiful," was the simple reflection of another.

Other examples of extended fellowship encouraged by the week include individual initiatives to open their gardens, host meals, and arrange children's events, with an emphasis on inclusiveness. Invitations to others to share meals and hospitality have a long history, of course–I can barely count the number of occasions that I've been welcomed by Jewish, Sikh, Hindu and other friends to celebrate fellowship involving food.

At a municipal level, many city administrations have invested energy and funding in interfaith projects.

In Bolton, UK, for example, the Bolton Interfaith Council brings together representatives from the three main faith groups in the city and other community members to "promote harmony, understanding, and co-operation between all members of the Bolton community"[11]. It has organized various events and projects, including a Young Ambassadors initiative, and a networking forum, and works with schools and community organisations.

In another English town, Southend-on-Sea in Essex, the Southend Interfaith Working Group has organized interfaith fairs and has agreed on a charter to encourage and strengthen friendship and cooperation among the town's many faith communities.

Some initiatives driven by individuals and small groups have also gained traction. The annual Interfaith Music Festival, *Faiths In Tune*, for example, was begun in 2011 by politics student Anja Fahlenkamp as a one-off event for students at SOAS, University of London. The Festival now attracts large numbers of the public, in well-supported events staged at prominent venues in London, Berlin, and New York.

Initiatives of this kind illustrate the varied and admirable efforts of individuals and organisations to foster friendship and co-operation, as well as to educate others about their often misunderstood positions.

The need for children to be educated about different faith traditions and worldviews has also received attention during recent years in some countries and states, where previously, strong or exclusive emphasis was put on teaching about state-endorsed or prevailing religions. Such teaching has become all-the-more important at a time of polarisation, the rise of nationalist and exclusivist politics in some countries, and a tendency to make generalised assumptions about some traditions.

The school curricula for Religious Education now encourages learning about, learning from, and fostering respect for other religions, practices, and values. Such teaching is mandated in some countries, such as in England [10]), the Republic of Ireland and South Africa.

Elsewhere, notably in France and Japan, teaching in moral values is offered in place of specific religious education. Such teaching also finds common ground with optional courses taught at more senior levels in ethics and philosophy, which aim to aid free thinking and encourage deep questioning.

Such policies can be seen as being positive, although remain limited in coverage, and often allowing opt-outs for specifically religious schools (e.g. in Malaysia, where Muslim students are taught Islamic Studies, while others must take Moral Studies).

Religious leaders have not been idle in reaching out to their peers from other traditions. The 'Great Commission' that many see as their purpose to evangelise and make converts to their own beliefs has not gone away, but the perceived need for focusing on this, at least among pluralists and many inclusivists, has reduced, as individuals have accepted that the 'One God' may be known by different names and be encountered in different ways.

The religious commentator and journalist Alan Race suggests that the response of religious leaders in recent decades has followed a twin-track approach, at least in the Christian tradition. One track has attempted to justify engagement and acceptance of others' views by theology; the other has seen a change in the way that faith can be deepened and experienced through engagement with others.

So, in the case of the second track, the work of the Trappist monk Father Thomas Keating to revitalize a practice of Christian meditation and prayer that was popular during the Middle Ages was inspired in no small part by recognizing a growing interest in Eastern meditation practices among people in the West.

Keating is among several who have embraced the wisdom of Eastern teachings, inviting representatives of Eastern faiths to the monastery of which he was abbot. Keating went on to help establish the Snowmass Interreligious Conference, and became an active member of the Temple of Understanding and the Monastic Interreligious Dialogue

The well-known Catholic theologian Thomas Merton, who travelled extensively in Asia, is another who has helped bridge Eastern and Western traditions, as is Bede Griffiths, who established a Christian ashram in India. The renown Zen master and friend of Merton, Thich Nhat Hanh, and Hindu and Gurdjieff follower Ravi Ravindra exemplify a growing number of teachers from Eastern traditions who have often couched their writings in terms of Christian teaching.

Hanh's book 'Living Buddha, Living Christ' teaches that Christians and Buddhists should emulate the lives of Jesus and the Buddha. From his sensitive consideration of the conversations that Jesus and the Buddha might have had were they to meet, Hanh concludes, "I do not think there is that much difference between Christians and Buddhists. Most of the boundaries we have created between our two traditions are artificial. Truth has no boundaries. Our differences may be mostly differences in emphasis"[12].

Reflecting on his scholarly interpretation of St. John's Gospel, meantime, Ravindra notes how he became convinced that "The major division in the human psyche is not horizontal or regional, dividing the Eastern from the Western soul, but rather vertical and global, separating the few from the many, and the spiritual, inner, and symbolical way of understanding from the material, outer, and literal one– culturally as well as in each human soul"[13].

We might also mention the current Dalai Lama, who when asked, "What is the best religion?" replied, "That set of beliefs and practices that help you become a kinder, more compassionate person"[14].

The teaching of the charismatic peacemaker Archbishop Desmond Tutu, a great friend of the Dalai Lama, also stresses the same point. Tutu's book

'God is not a Christian' expresses a strongly pluralist viewpoint: "Accidents of birth and geography determine to a very large extent to what faith we belong," he notes. "The chances are very great that if you were born in Pakistan, you are Muslim, or Hindu if you happen to be born in India, or a Shintoist if it is Japan, and a Christian if you are born in Italy"[15].

He goes on: "To claim God exclusively for Christians is to make God too small and in a real sense is blasphemous. God is bigger than Christianity and cares for more than Christians only. He has to, if only for the simple reason that Christians are quite late arrivals on the world scene. God has been around since even before creation, and that is a very long time. If God's love is limited to Christians, what must the fate be of all who existed before Christ?"[16].

We could easily extend this list of well-known, highly esteemed religious leaders and exemplars, who stress the complementarity between their faiths rather than their differences.

Religious bodies have themselves taken great strides toward recognizing and honouring the faiths of others. In the Roman Catholic Church, a movement toward toleration and dialogue became palpable with the decrees of the Vatican II Council, which deliberated on doctrinal matters over three years during the 1960s.

Theologian Paul F. Knitter, who acted as a translator during this extended series of debates, sums up what was a truly radical shift in position for the Church: "[The Council] was writing about the value

Clive Johnson

of other religions, about God's presence in other religions, a clear statement that even if they are atheists, if they are following their ethics, they are heir to eternal life"[17].

The increasing number of theologians aligning themselves with a pluralist position has also strengthened the need for interfaith practitioners. Knitter describes his dialogue with members of other faiths as being the most important influence for him[18].

However, in many parts of the world, as well as within faith bodies themselves, pluralism and inclusivism have not been welcomed.

Even some apparently well-intended initiatives in more liberal countries to engage with people from other faiths have resulted in a sharp backlash. In early 2017, a reading from The *Qur'an* at a service at an Anglican Cathedral in Glasgow triggered angry responses from Christians (a reading in Arabic, by a Muslim student, that included the Islamic teaching that Jesus is not the son of God and should not be worshipped).

Beyond widespread criticism on social media, clergy themselves rebuked the decision to allow this reading from a church pulpit. The former bishop of Rochester, Michael Nazir-Ali, said: "Christians should know what their fellow citizens believe...This is not, however, the same thing as having it read in church in the context of public worship. The authorities of the Scottish Episcopal Church should immediately repudiate this ill-advised invitation and exercise appropriate discipline for those involved"[19].

Two years earlier, a Muslim prayer event hosted at a church in Waterloo, London, received strong criticism from Anglican clergy. By allowing this consecrated space to be used, and himself offering a prayer to Allah (the Arabic Christian word for God), the pastor responsible, Canon Giles Goddard, was accused of breaking canon law and bringing the church into disrepute. He later issued an apology for allowing a non-Christian act of worship within the church sanctuary[20].

Episodes of this kind are a reminder that those who offer platforms to people of other faiths need to be sensitive to their own communities' particular beliefs when such invitations involve pronouncements or acts of worship in a consecrated space that might be out of keeping with the teachings and structures of their tradition.

Shared worship may not be problematic when addressing general teachings, such as a theme like compassion, but risks causing offence to those whose faith is rooted in a specific creed when an apparent contradiction or denial of these beliefs is proffered by those who believe otherwise.

However, we shouldn't give up hope that the particularity problem might preclude an opportunity for inter-religious cooperation. As Pope Francis said during a meeting with Buddhist, Hindu, Muslim and Christian communities on a visit to Sri Lanka:

"Inter-religious dialogue...must be grounded in a full and forthright presentation of our respective convictions. Certainly, such dialogue will accentuate how varied our beliefs, traditions and practices are. But if we are honest in presenting our convictions, we will be able to see more clearly what we hold in common. New avenues will be opened for mutual esteem, cooperation and indeed friendship"[21].

Interfaith Ministry

One response to the growth of interest in an interfaith ethos outside of established religion has been the creation of seminaries that have the express purpose of training interfaith ministers.

We've already mentioned the pioneering work of Rabbi Joseph Gelberman, who founded The New Seminary for Interfaith Studies in New York. Gelberman dedicated himself to interfaith working while remaining passionate in his work as a rabbi, later becoming president of All Faiths Seminary International, which he also founded.

His work inspired the creation in the mid-1990's of an interfaith seminary in London, which has evolved into what is now the One Spirit Interfaith Foundation. Together, both these and other schools have now taught several thousand ministers.

Ministry is a much misunderstood term. Anyone who is open to being guided by what they see as being divine, and who makes themselves available to serve others, performs a ministry. A musician, care

Understanding Interfaith

worker, listening friend, and nurse are all ministers—no dog collar or fancy hat are required.

A minister is one who helps another connect with the Source greater than themselves that brings guidance, comfort, and joy—whether or not this is consciously recognized as being divine by those receiving ministry.

Ceremony, prayer, counselling may all play a part in this. However, ministry is more about an attitude toward life, the readiness to offer whatever gifts have been given to a minister. If it's true, as I believe, that we are all connected through one common spirit, and this spirit is nothing less than God in action, then we all have the capacity to be ministers to each other.

The work of interfaith ministers is gaining popularity, as people have become more interested in spirituality, have fallen out of love with organized religion, or are questioning its relevance for them today. Those who serve under an interfaith pennant have an important role to play.

This ministry is still in its infancy and is rarely manifested as regular worship or organized gatherings (although there are such groups). Interfaith ministers don't have pastoral care for flocks or congregations, nor have prescribed responsibilities or an institutionally-determined focus for their ministries.

While it is still largely outside of the mainstream, there remains a long distance to go in promoting awareness, explaining what interfaith ministry is, and whom it may be relevant for.

Into the new age

Beyond shifts of focus in seminary, institutional and academic circles, the broadly defined 'new age movement' has also engaged a revival in interest in Earth-based practices that honour the sacredness of all life on Earth.

Many alternative ways of expressing spirituality, and for making sense of life's purpose through expanding levels of consciousness and awareness of the limitations of normal human interpretations of reality, have taken form within this movement.

While individuals who express their spirituality in such ways often form into groups with others of like mind, even within well structured and established organisations (such as is the case of the Order of Bards, Ovates and Druids), an adherence to dogma and fixed statements of belief tends to be less prescribed than is usually witnessed in most traditional religions.

The number of individuals who practice new expressions of so-called 'new spirituality' is certainly growing. The extensive consultative exercise *Spiritualise*[22] of the RSA [11] in the UK highlighted a trend toward new expressions of spirituality, often not placing any dependence on membership of a particular institution.

Channelled teachings and revelations to individuals acting as scribes have also found new audiences. *A Course In Miracles* is one example of such transcriptions that have attracted millions of followers worldwide. This self-study program, scribed by Helen Schucman, offers a means for inquiring deeply into key questions concerning life, reality, and divinity, but without needing to align with a church or other religious institution. Neal Donald Walsh's transcribed *Conversations with God* numbers among other such writings.

Encouragingly, many people who align themselves with an interfaith mindset stress the need to allow each individual to follow their path–which of course may include a traditional religion. One thing that interfaith is not about is challenging the established order. On the contrary, those who adopt an interfaith mindset are keen to draw on the several thousand years' of wisdom, expressed through countless stories, scriptures, and the teachings of renown sages, all of which are more widely accessible to us than has ever been the case before.

Interfaith and the individual

My sense is that, if an interfaith ethos is gathering momentum, it's largely achieving this at the level of the individual, and this movement isn't hitting the headlines. It is for individuals to take the initiative to organize themselves, to find their own *sanghas*, to mix and match from what they read, hear, and experience, according to what appeals to them. This is a promising response to meeting the demands of new expressions of spirituality, but is not without its problems, as we'll see in the final chapter.

At an individual level, the consequence of many decades of cultures meeting is perhaps best illustrated through the prevalence of interfaith partnerships. In an extensive 2010 survey, former Wall Street Journal editor Naomi Schaefer Riley found that 42% of marriages in the US were between people professing different faiths[23]. This demographic is not restricted to large cities, where it might be thought that there's a greater tendency for people from different backgrounds to come together: the pattern is repeated across the country, and transcends factors such as individuals' educational and income levels.

This same survey revealed that more than a quarter of people in interfaith marriages had changed their native religion, while many of these confirmed that they had gained a more favourable impression of others' faiths as a result of marriage.

A further survey, conducted by the author Erika B. Seamon for her book 'Interfaith marriage in America: The transformation of religion and Christianity,' similarly reports that respondents claim that their marriages have been enhanced as a result of their faith differences[24].

I think this finding is staggering–at least in the USA, close to 50% of married couples are now in interfaith partnerships. According to another survey[25], this compares with just 19% that married before 1960, and relates to a population that in 2014 declared itself to be 70% Christian[26].

We must be careful when interpreting such statistics, of course–for example, the surveys referred to exclude divorced couples from their data. However, a strong trend toward interfaith partnerships, and in turn, families, is nonetheless clearly apparent.

In many countries, however, interfaith weddings do not yet carry legal status. Individuals must separately apply for a marriage licence, usually via a civil registrar. But even this legacy of state-endorsed religion is changing in some countries. Interfaith weddings can be legally solemnised in Scotland and Republic of Ireland, for example, and a movement to allow the same in England and Wales is under government review.

Expressions of interfaith can't be easily boxed, and aren't always obvious. Education and exposure to diverse worldviews are helping to reveal the extent of such expressions, but it's hard to form an accurate picture.

With this in mind, we might now turn to consider what responses might be appropriate in meeting the emergence of a powerful, if still patchy and fledgling, interfaith movement.

Clive Johnson

CHAPTER 5

How should we respond?

WE CONCLUDED THE previous chapter with an intention to explore a possible response to the massive growth in interfaith interest. I labelled this trend a 'movement,' for want of an alternative description. I suggest such a label to describe the strong tide of common interest that is prompting direct participation as a response, even if such responses happen independently of each other, and may take on different forms.

Such a labelling seems appropriate to me, given the fact that there have been many responses to changing patterns of belief and practice among different faith communities.

So we might ask whether anything new might the done to fully embrace the 'Interfaith age.' I suggest that this question might be explored regarding who might offer a response:

- How might we respond as faith bodies?
- How should we respond as individuals, at the grass-roots? and
- How might society respond?

Further, we might build upon these different perspectives by considering whether there might be a place for promoting a new 'interfaith' religion.

How might we respond as faith bodies?

My sense is that there isn't a need for anything specifically new, at least among those institutions that take pluralism and inclusivism seriously, even if there's always scope for doing more of what is already happening. The evidence of interfaith weeks, shared pulpits, and earnest inter-religious dialogue described in the previous chapter suggests that, at least in some parts of the world, bold steps in interfaith engagement have already been taken.

Ever closer cooperation between representatives of different faiths, the will to not only tolerate and respect but also to be open to learning from those of who express their spirituality outside the framework of organized religion, and an overwhelming focus on the principles of belief that unite rather than separate people of different traditions, will help to strengthen this movement.

Certainly, there must always be scope for more widespread education about interfaith initiatives, and we might hope that faith community leaders will increasingly encourage their congregations to explore the faith expressions of others.

Encouragingly, the evidence of the 2008 survey for the Parliament of the World's Religions suggests that substantial progress has been made in this direction.

How should we respond as individuals, at the grass-roots?

One possible picture that might emerge in the coming years is one of faith experience that isn't largely dominated by the main five or six traditions. Rather, many million different ways for expressing spirituality and connecting with The Divine may take precedence, with individuals working out ways for celebrating and practising their faith, rather than being strongly guided by institutions and dogma.

This picture would fit very well with what we might include under the 'interfaith' heading. This extends beyond a sharing of views, experiences, and actions among peoples of different religions, to recognizing that every individual can work out their relationship with their God in their unique way.

Celebrating difference, joining where there is common ground, and seeking inspiration from the teachings of several faith traditions and other inspired sources might feature strongly.

There must be scope for building communities of people who follow different spiritual paths, including for organized worship and regular fellowship or sangha. Many such initiatives may often remain isolated and grass-roots ventures, lack funding and visibility to gather momentum on a regional, national, or international basis. However, this shouldn't dilute their value.

One approach to recognizing and embracing interfaith principles in a common practice of worship and fellowship is a gathering that avoids putting labels on concepts like 'God,' and which aims to be fully inclusive of every individual.

The Universalist Unitarian Church comes close to this model, although some Universalists have clearer views about who God is than others. Independent churches have also come into being.

One example is Spirit United, a spiritual community based in St.Paul, Minnesota, who I had the pleasure to visit recently. Its stated mission sums up its commitment to different traditions:

> *"Our Spirit United is a community and center where people gather to unfold spiritually, to awaken more fully as whole beings connecting to the Oneness of The Divine and all of creation. We offer and support events, gatherings, and celebrations for individuals to adventure in self-discovery*

and leadership. We integrate universal and ancient spiritual practices and traditions for healing and transforming our souls. We practice being whole within a supportive and caring community as we merge the past, present, and future into today's world"[1].

Its spiritual teachings embrace diversity, honouring individual's spiritual paths, and drawing on the wisdom of many traditions, including respect for the Earth. Guest speakers from various traditions feature prominently in its Sunday meetings.

Interfaith Minister Steven Greenebaum is among others who have established their own interfaith communities. The church that he began, the Living Interfaith Church in Lynnwood, Washington, brings together Muslims, Jews, Christians, Humanists, Buddhists and Baha'i into a single, active congregation. In his book 'The Interfaith Alternative, Embracing Spiritual Diversity,' Greenebaum explains that this is a community that "celebrates our diversity, covenanting to nurture and support as well as respect one another."[2]

Active spiritual community, led by a covenant and shared assumptions, is central to the paradigm for interfaith worship that Greenebaum advocates. He suggests that different spiritual paths can serve as guides but not ends[3], and that tolerating each other is not enough–members of an interfaith community must honour and celebrate each other's uniquely personal ways of connecting with The Divine[4].

These are noble objectives, and recognizing the importance for individuals to pursue their own paths within a congregation that honours and supports them. Crucially though, each individual's spiritual path needs to have substance, which they may or may not find beyond the well-defined teachings and practices of an established faith tradition.

How might society respond?

Few would disagree that the way a society recognizes the value of religion and the degree to which it tolerates the freedom of its citizens to practice different beliefs has a profound affect on how it functions and develops.

In many Western societies, tolerating and integrating different faith groups has for a long time been fundamental in government strategies, especially in countries whose ethnic profile is very diverse. While still strong in some parts of the world, state-sponsored religion is less of a force than it once was, while some societies (notably France) have recognized the separation of state and religious affairs for more than a century.

If participation in faith-based communities is important for teaching and encouraging sound moral behaviours and promoting concern for the common man, then societies might have reason to be concerned when membership and allegiance to traditional faith groups are declining.

Multicultural societies, in which interfaith marriage, agnosticism, and pro-spiritual or anti-religious allegiances are prevalent, need to take seriously how they accommodate the perspectives of the many in shaping the spiritual life of a nation. This, of course, includes embracing those who pursue a multi- or inter-faith spiritual path, alongside established faith traditions.

Initiatives such as the UK RSA's *Spiritualise* project have highlighted the need for public discourse and action on such matters[5]. This extensive consultation exercise concluded that many people acknowledge that there is a spiritual aspect to their lives, but don't really know what this means. Taking the view that the solution to many social problems requires us to "do depth" in public, the project stresses the need for governments, institutions, and individuals to engage with these spiritual roots.

Such initiatives can have great value, but only if they are widely acknowledged and acted upon. More of the same is needed to help raise discussion in society, involving many different voices, and in a more objective and inclusive way than (for example) churches have debated their declining congregations and crises of views on matters such as women bishops and blessing same-sex weddings.

There is obvious potential for interfaith advocates to help shape and even lead such debate. In turn, the importance to wider society of the matters discussed and proposals made need to be given prominence, through promotion and lobbying government and other relevant bodies.

Is there a need for a new religion?

In the sense that we've defined it, interfaith refers to communication, cooperation, and action between individuals who come from different faith traditions, and who typically connect with The Divine and express their spirituality in different ways. It *doesn't* refer to a single system of belief, one which may draw upon or attempt to align the teachings of several faiths.

Nonetheless, a trend toward recognizing commonality between faiths that's an important consequence of interfaith dialogue does call into question whether it might be desirable for a single 'multifaith' to take prominence in societies that have already provided a melting pot of people from diverse cultures, or whether indeed this might be the ultimate destination for those who come together with an interfaith focus.

There already is at least one religion that synthesises the teachings of multiple faiths, Ba'hai.

Bahá'u'lláh, born in nineteenth century Iran, and seen as the messenger of the faith, scribed thousands of verses, letters, and books. These teach that all faith traditions come from the same source, with each effectively being a fresh chapter in the continuing revelation of divinity. The overriding message of the faith

Understanding Interfaith

is that all people should work together for unity, recognizing other faiths as being true and valid.

There are now around 6 million Bahá'ís in the world, spread across 235 countries. This number is obviously small compared with 'The big six' traditions and hardly suggests a groundswell movement, although one source records the Baha'i Faith as being the second fastest growing religion in the world[6] [12].

The principle tenets of the faith are ones that are common to other traditions, including:

- There is one, omnipotent God
- The purpose of human life is to grow spiritually, ultimately coming fully into the presence and radiance of God
- The boundless beauty and richness of all forms of life are manifestations of divinity.

Prayer, meditation, and studying the writings of Bahá'u'lláh and other Bahá'í leaders, form an essential part of Bahá'í devotion.

However, Bahá'ís have also adopted practices that are particular to their faith: for example, turning toward the shrine of the Bahá'u'lláh' in prayer, which they also strive to visit at least once during their lifetime. The global community is administered by a system of institutions, each with its defined sphere of action, and local communities gather for a feast every nineteen days.

Still, these are light concessions to the inevitable need for organizing a large community compared with most traditions. Bahá'í worship services have no sermon, rituals, sacraments, or clergy. The Bahá'í community has very few houses of worship (physical buildings), while each Bahá'í is free to choose his or her approach to meditation. Music used for devotion is similarly suited to individual or cultural preference. The primary focus of Ba'hai is on our relationship with God.

Is Ba'hai a faith that transcends all other traditions, or is it rather the most recent revelation that honours but adds to earlier teachings–in the same way that Muslims understand Islam as a new and superior revelation to Christianity?

How this question is answered is, of course, a matter of perspective. Still, the fact that Ba'hai is available for anyone who would want to be a member of a unifying faith suggests to me that there's no urgent need for creating a new religion. Excepting one that codifies its beliefs and organizes itself in other ways, it's hard to see how this might offer anything new.

The movement toward new expressions of spirituality through fellowships such as Spirit United and the Living Interfaith Church might prevail during the coming decades, but I don't believe that this is–or should be–a call to create a new, unified religion. Indeed, these churches provide a space for individuals from different faith paths to come together, rather than advocating a single, new faith that draws on multifaith teachings.

Speaking back in the nineteenth century with reference to religious conflicts, theologian Josiah Royce remarked, "It is useless to reduce the many to the one merely by wiping out the many. It is useless to make some new sect whose creed shall be that there are no sects. The unity of the visible church, under any one creed, or with any one settled system of religious practices, is an unattainable and undesirable ideal. The varieties of religious experience in James's sense [13] of that term are endless. The diversity of gifts is as great as is the diversity of strong and loyal personalities."[7]

This appears to be the position taken at the 2007 gathering of forty-five religious leaders and scholars in Monterrey, Mexico, referred to earlier. The conference concluded that it doesn't view the creation of a single global institution or representative council for all religions as being desirable: "The difficulty with this concept," the gathering asserted[8], "is that there are in existence a good number of interfaith organizations that are global in their aspirations.... The direct result of this ambition has been to create intense competition between international organizations, vying for association with the U.N., funding, and the participation of important religious leaders, as well as publicity and general support".

Notably, the gathering also expressed concern at the growing "emphasis on 'spirituality' rather than 'religion'," which it says, "presents a challenge to all those who deal primarily in terms of official representation and the historical religions"[9].

The report noted that "charges of facile universalism, shallow individualism, syncretism, and dilettantism can readily be brought against 'religionless' spiritual seekers", but went on to say that "Study and sharing of contemplative practices [and the inner experience] is one important and serious element in the interfaith movement, and the spiritual dimension more generally continues to provide much momentum"[10].

The distinction between stressing spirituality, which might be perfectly in keeping within an interfaith community, but doing so in a 'religionless' way deserves some attention.

One difficulty with pursuing a lone spiritual path is that this often involves growing in isolation from others, while lacking spiritual rooting in a clear set of scriptures or other readings, and without easy access to a spiritual director or elder who fully understands their path.

For someone who has established depth in their path through meditation and prayer, and who is closely in touch with The Divine, this may not be a problem. The risk is for the many who have not discovered this relationship, or who waver in committing to the spiritual practices that would give them this connection.

Community–*sangha*–and the guidance of trusted elders who can offer relevant teaching and counsel, matter. These may be available to a degree in communities such as the Living Interfaith Church, but cannot easily cater for those who are embarking on a new spiritual quest, nor necessarily for those whose unique path is leading them in a direction that might be unfamiliar to others with whom they associate.

Unless it is well rooted, being 'religionless' can also risk the problem of "digging too many wells". I use this analogy with reference to a wonderful collection of teachings from many traditions, compiled by the American priest and theologian Matthew Fox under the title 'One River, Many Wells'[11].

The essential idea expressed by Fox is that there is a single Source (God), but Who or Which can be accessed by many different traditions. Each well needs to be dug deeply to tap into the flowing waters of the one river (Source); to start 'digging' too many wells, or dipping into too many different teachings, means that our understanding of The Divine will always remain shallow.

Rev. Dr. Gavin Ashenden, an Anglican priest and theologian, eluded to this risk in a recent radio interview[12]. Ashenden argues that interfaith communities can take a spiritual seeker so far, being a "good first base," as he puts it. However, any individual who takes their spiritual path seriously ultimately needs to make a choice about which road to follow: to adopt the particular teachings of Jesus, for example, or to dedicate a life to understanding the teachings of the Buddha. For those who take an exclusivist view, there can be no alternative when reaching this crossroad.

Should then each individual take responsibility for their spiritual path, or is it preferable to pursue a spiritual inquiry with the support, practices, and teachings of a well-defined and well-established tradition? Can interfaith communities such as Spirit United offer sufficient substance in their teaching, or depth in their fellowship, than groups of individuals who subscribe to a common creed? Should an open-minded spiritual seeker be advised to align with an established faith tradition, rather than with an interfaith fellowship?

These are perhaps questions that each individual needs to answer for themselves. Interfaith is a powerful and necessary force in our world, but perhaps it's one that doesn't and never should seek to replace or denigrate the many and great traditions that are the spiritual home for billions of God-loving, peace-loving, and people-loving human beings.

Notes

[1] *Kirtan*: Non-denominational singing, originating from India.

[2] I use the term the 'big six' to refer to the leading faith traditions that are practiced in most parts of the world, as measured by their number of adherents: Christianity, Islam, Hinduism, Buddhism, Sikhism, Judaism. This excludes some traditions whose following is largely restricted to a single culture or region, such as Juche and Chinese traditional religion (Confucianism).

[3] Today there are 192 member states of the United Nations, including former states that have divided, been ceded with others, or changed their name since the UN's foundation.

[4] Mantra-based meditation is not an exclusively 'owned' practice of Hindus, Buddhists, or any other faith, even if it does have a much longer tradition in India than in the West.

[5] Several faith traditions, not least, Pagan and Druid traditions, have codified a view of the Earth is an organism into a diverse number of faith practices.

Clive Johnson

[6] The lovingkindness prayer, also known as the *Metta Sutta* or *Karaniya Metta Sutta*, is a teaching attributed to the Buddha that encourages a development of pure love for the self to pure love for all beings.

[7] Ahura Mazda is the creator and sole God of Zoroastrianism.

[8] The notion that we each have a soul is rejected by some Buddhists, who believe that nothing exists between the lower self and Pure Ultimate Consciousness. However, *Atta* is generally interpreted by most Buddhists today as being equivalent to the self or soul that other religions speak of when referring to the (spiritual) aspect of a person that transcends the physical body.

[9] The *Manu Smriti* is one of many Hindi Dharmasastras.

[10] Schools in England are required to provide Religious Education, although parents may request that their child is excluded from it.

[11] RSA: Royal Society for the encouragement of Arts, Manufactures and Commerce.

[12] The growth in Baha'i members is attributed largely to increases in India.

[13] Royce here refers to his contemporary and friend, William James, author of *Varieties of Religious Experiences*.

References

FRONTPIECE

1. *God is not a Christian: Speaking Truth in Times of Crisis* by Desmond Tutu, 2011, HarperOne, p6.

2. Statement from the Thirteenth Annual Meeting of the Indian Theological Association 1989, cited in *Religious Pluralism: An Indian Christian Perspective* by K. Pathil, 1991, ISPCK, Delhi.

3. *State of Interreligious Movement Report* by Jeff Israel (ed.), June 2008, Council for a Parliament of the World's Religions Publication, Brooklyn, NY, p 10.

1. WHY THE BIG FUSS?

1. *The Sources of Religious Insight* by Josiah Royce, 1912, The Trustees of Lake Forest University/ Charles Scribner's Sons, New York, pp2-3

2. Tutu, 2011, *op. cit.*

3. 'For the World's Sake...Unity' by Maxwell Craig in *For God's Sake...Unity: The Church is Called to be One* by Maxwell Craig (ed.), 2004, Wild Goose Publications, p 161.

2. WHAT IS INTERFAITH?

1. *Church of England Doctrine Commission Report: The Mystery of Salvation,* 1995, Church House Publishing, London, p184.

2. *The Purpose of Interfaith Dialogue* by Dr. Ataullah Siddiqui, The Markfield Institute of Higher Educa-

tion, Leicester, http://www.mihe.org.uk/the-purpose-of-interfaith-dialogue, accessed 5 March 2017.

3. Royce, 1912, *op. cit.*, pp2-3.

4. *ibid.*, p18.

5. *ibid.*, p125.

3. WHERE IS THE COMMON GROUND?

1. www.dailykos.com/story/2015/6/24/1395897/-Religion-101-What-is-Comparative-Religion.

2. *Religion: The Basics* by Malory Nye, 2012, Routledge, p3.

3. The British Humanist Society, quoted in 'The Golden Rule: Not So Golden Anymore' by Stephen Anderson, *Philosophy Now*, Feb/Mar 2017 Issue 118.

4. Notes on The Golden Rule, from *The Internet Encyclopedia of Philosophy*, http://www.iep.utm.edu/goldrule/ accessed 3 March 2017.

5. See *Man's Eternal Quest* by Paramahansa Yogananda, 2012, Yogananda Satsang Society of India, p18.

6. Quoted in *I AM THAT Dialogues of Sri Nisargadatta Maharaj*, p1, www.anandavala.info/miscl/I_Am_That.pdf, accessed 23 March 2017.

7. *Gates of Repentance: The New Union Prayerbook for the Days of Awe* by Chaim Stern (ed.), 1978 (third edition), Central Conference of American Rabbis.

8. See Paramahansa Yogananda, 2012, *op. cit.*, p18.

9. *I AM THAT Dialogues of Sri Nisargadatta Maharaj*, *op. cit.*, p1

10. *The Dawn-Breakers: Nabíl's Narrative of the Early Days of the Bahá'í Revelation* by Nabil, 1932, US Bahá'í Publishing Trust, p 316.

11. 'The Way of the Gods' by Tom Hamilton Hammond, www.truthmagazine.com/archives/volume34/GOT034141.html accessed 230317.

12. 'The Concept of Nirvana from a Psychological Point of View' by Dr. Ruwan M. Jayatunge MD, http://www.lakehouse.lk/mihintalava/buddhism10.htm, accessed 28 June 2017.

13. Attributed to The Buddha, See: *The Gospel of Buddha* by Paul Carus, 1894, p55, https://archive.org/details/gospelofbuddha008430mbp, accessed 28 June 2017.

14. A teaching of The Buddha, see Carus, 1894, Ch. 25., *op. cit.*

15. Quoted in *Ramkrishna* by Gajanan Khergamker, 2006, Jaico Publishing House.

16. Quoted in *The Sacred Pipe: Black Elk's Account of the Seven Rites of the Oglala Sioux* by Joseph Epes Brown (ed.), 1989 (new edition), University of Oklahoma Press, p 13.

17. *The Hymns of Atharvan Zarathushtra* by Jatindra Mohan Chatterji, 1967, pp 344 and 345, http://www.avesta.org/chatterj_opf_files accessed 28 June 2017.

18. *The Summons of the Lord of Hosts: Tablets of Bahá'u'lláh* by Bahaaullaah, Bahá'í Publishing, p130.

19. *Dhammapada–Sayings of the Buddha 1* by J. Richards (transl.), http://www.edepot.com/dhamma2.html accessed 28 June 2017.

20. Quoted in 'The Best: 72+ African Wise Proverbs and Inspiring Quotes', *Afritorial*, June 22, 2012, www.afritorial.com/the-best-72-african-wise-proverbs/ accessed 230317.

21. Traditional repentance verse from *The Practices and Vows of Samantabadra Bodhisattva*, Avatamsaka Sutra, Ch. 40.

22. Cited in *Seventy Thousand Veils* by Claire Porter, 2010, O Books, p 113.

23. *Anguttara Nikaya* I–103.

24. 'The Way of the Gods' by Tom Hamilton Hammond, http://www.truthmagazine.com/archives/volume34/GOT034141.html accessed 230317.

25. Israel (ed.), 2008, *op. cit.*, pp 5-6.

26. *Prayers of the Cosmos, Meditations on the Aramaic Words of Jesus* by Neil Douglas-Klotz, 1990, Harper & Row.

27. Cited in *Oneness: Great Principles Shared by All Religions* by Jeffrey Moses, 2002 (reprint edition), Ballantine Books, p 76.

4. HOW IS INTERFAITH PLAYING OUT TODAY?

1. *The Mystic Heart: Discovering a Universal Spirituality in the World's Religions* by Wayne Teasdale, 1999, New World Library, Novato, CA, p4.

2. *The Great Transformation* by Karen Armstrong, 2005, Atlantic.

3. Karen Armstrong, in an interview with *The Independent*, www.independent.co.uk/arts-entertainment/books/features/karen-armstrong-exploring-the-common-ground-between-the-worlds-great-religions-470137.html accessed 20 March 2017.

4. Cited by Rabbi Rami I Mark Shapiro, 'Moving the Fence: One Rabbi's View of Inter-religious Dialogue,' *Inter-religious Dialogue: Voices from a New Frontier* by M. Darrol Bryant and Frank Flinn (eds.), 1989, Paragon House, New York, p 33.

5. *Declaration on the Elimination of All Forms of Intolerance and of Discrimination Based on Religion or Belief*, United Nations, 25 November 1981.

6. 'Pluralism—A Home For All Of Us' by Paul Chaffee, https://www.parliamentofreligions.org/content/pluralism-home-all-us accessed 28 March 2015.

7. 'Why Interfaith Dialogue?' By Abdul Malik Mujahid, https://parliamentofreligions.org/content/why-interfaith-dialogue-0 accessed 28 March 2017.

8. Israel (ed.), 2008, *op. cit.*

9. Israel (ed.), 2008, *op. cit.*, p8.

10. www.worldinterfaithharmonyweek.com, accessed 26 June 2017

11. www.boltoninterfaithcouncil.org.uk, accessed 26 June 2017.

12. *Living Buddha, Living Christ* by Thich Nhat Hanh, 1996, Rider, p154.

13. *The gospel of John in the light of Indian mysticism* by Ravi Ravindra, 2004, Inner Traditions, Rochester, VT, p1.

14. Quoted in 'Is There a Common Ground between Buddhism and Islam?' by Dr. Alexander Berzin https://studybuddhism.com/en/advanced-studies/history-culture/buddhism-islam/is-there-a-common-ground-between-buddhism-and-islam, accessed 21 June 2017.

15. Tutu, 2011, *op. cit.*, p5.

16. Tutu, 2011, *op. cit.*, p14.

17. Quoted in Chaffee, 2015, *op. cit.*

18. *Introducing Theologies of Religions* by Paul F. Knitter, 2002, Orbis, Maryknoll, NY, p4.

19. 'Bishop 'Distressed' by Row Following Qur'an Reading at Cathedral,' https://www.theguardian.com/uk-news/2017/jan/15/st-marys-cathedral-glasgow-quran-reading-david-chillingworth accessed 21 June 2017.

20. See 'Muslim Prayers in Church of England Parish' by John Bingham, 13 March 2015, *Daily Telegraph*.

21. *Catholic Herald* Tuesday, 13 Jan 2015, http://www.catholicherald.co.uk/news/2015/01/13/pope-francis-speech-to-inter-religious-meeting-in-sri-lanka/ accessed 25 June 2017.

22. *Spiritualise: Revitalising Spirituality to Address 21st Century Challenges*, RSA, 2014, https://www.thersa.org/discover/publications-and-articles/reports/spiritualise-revitalising-spirituality-to-address-21st century-challenges accessed 10 March 2017.

23. 'Seven things you don't know about interfaith marriage' by Naomi Schaefer Riley, Published 19 April 2013, Fox News, www.foxnews.com/opinion/

Understanding Interfaith

2013/04/19/seven-things-dont-know-about-interfaith-marriage.html, accessed 26 June 2017.

24. Cited in 'Interfaith Marriage in America: Past and Future' by Susan Katz Miller, *Huffington Post*, 14 March 2013, http://www.huffingtonpost.com/susan-katz-miller/interfaith-marriage-in-america-past-and-future_b_2875060.html.

25. 'America's Changing Religious Landscape,' Pew Research Center, 2015, http://www.pewforum.org/religious-landscape-study/, accessed 23 June 2017.

26. 'America's Changing Religious Landscape,' 2015, *op. cit.*

5. HOW SHOULD WE RESPOND?

1. Spirit United website, http://www.spiritunited.com/about-us/guiding-principles accessed 23 June 2017.

2. *The Interfaith Alternative, Embracing Spiritual Diversity* by Steven Greenebaum, 2012, New Society Publishers, Gabriola Island, BC, p116.

3. Greenebaum, 2012, *op. cit.*, p96.

4. Greenebaum, 2012, *op. cit.*, p62.

5. RSA, 2014, *op. cit.*

6. World Christian Database, Gordon-Conwell Theological Seminary, quoted in Baha'i Rants, http://bahairants.com/second-fastest-growing-religion-115.html, published 1 April 2008, accessed 22 June 2017.

7. Royce, 1912, *op. cit.*, pp133-134.

8. Israel (ed.), 2008, *op. cit.*, p 6.

9. Israel (ed.), 2008, *op. cit.*, p 7.

10. Israel (ed.), 2008, *op. cit.*, p244.

11. *One River, Many Wells: Wisdom Springing from Global Faiths* by Matthew Fox, 2004, Tarcherperigee.

12. Rev. Dr. Gavin Ashenden, interview in *Beyond Belief*, 'Interfaith Worship,' BBC Radio 4, http://www.bbc.co.uk/programmes/b08j9z6j broadcast 20 March 2017.

Understanding Interfaith

Terminology

Agnostic. Someone who is doubtful or not committed to the idea of God's existence, believing that this cannot be proved.

Comparative Religion. The study of the origins, development of, similarities and differences of the practices and dogmas of world religions.

Core. The heart or true essence of a person (see also Self).

Creed. A defined set of beliefs about the nature of divinity.

Denomination. An organized religious group whose dogma and practises may vary from others who hold to the same faith tradition.

(The) Divine. Universal term for God, or Source of All Being. A power or essence that transcends human understanding, which is greater than, and contains everything, and which exists outside of time. May be represented by one or many deities and be described by many different names.

Divinity. Relating to The Divine.

Dogma. A set of beliefs or doctrines that are proclaimed by a religious body as being true.

Earth-based Tradition. A faith tradition that worships nature, holding that all life is related and sustained by a cosmic consciousness. Shamanic, Pagan, Native American, Wicca, Shinto, and Druid faiths number among Earth-based traditions.

Eastern / Western Tradition. Generalised term to distinguish the major thought systems that have alternatively developed and prevailed in Eastern and Western cultures. The former include Indic and Asian traditions; the latter Christian and neo-Pagan faiths.

Ecumenical. An initiative or desire to embrace unity among all denominations of a particular faith tradition. Typically applied when speaking about the "Christian Church," or efforts to bring Christians from different sects or denominations into partnership.

Exclusivism. A belief that only the position maintained by a particular faith is true and valid. Christian exclusivists maintain that salvation can only be achieved by accepting Jesus Christ as saviour.

Faith. Individual trust in a personal belief, usually rooted in a spiritual conviction and not being capable of rational proof.

Faith Tradition. A single religion, mythology, or way of comprehending and relating to The Divine. Examples include Christianity, Buddhism, and Islam, while each may be represented by several separate denominations.

God. An alternative term for The Divine.

Inclusivism. A belief that, while one faith path may be superior or preferred over others, other traditions can lead to encounters with The Divine, and speak certain truths.

Interfaith. Communication, co-operation, and shared worship between people of different faiths. Interfaith initiatives recognize that there is much commonality in what is taught by alternative traditions, honouring

Understanding Interfaith

the alternative ways that individuals have for celebrating and connecting with The Divine.

Liturgy. A set form of practices for public worship.

Multifaith. A practice or belief that involves and maintains the validity of more than one faith tradition. This is distinct from *interfaith*, which recognizes and respects alternative beliefs (see above).

Myth. A story or way of explaining typically important and profound truths that have been passed down within a particular culture. In one sense, all stories and explanations offered in religious scriptures are myths that speak to followers of a particular tradition (thus, the *Genesis* myth explains the origins of the world in a way that's meaningful for Jews, Christians, and Muslims).

Nirvana. A transcendent, selfless state in which there is no suffering or continued enslavement to the cycle of death and rebirth. Nirvana is the ultimate state sought by Buddhists.

Pantheism. Identification with or worship of Divinity by many gods or multiple representations of The Divine. Contrasts with monotheistic faiths, which recognize a single deity.

Perennial Tradition / Perennial Philosophy. A belief that all the world's religions offer the same underlying teaching. As Richard Rohr puts it, "each tradition continues to say, in their own way: there is a Divine Reality underneath and inherent in the world of things, there is in the human soul a natural capacity, similarity, and longing for this Divine Reality, [and] the final goal of all existence is union with this Divine Reality" (Father Richard Rohr in *Oneing* 1(1)

Spring 2003, Editor's Note, The Center for Action and Contemplation / The Rohr Institute).

Pluralism. A belief that there is more than one path that leads to God. Pluralists advocate tolerance of all faith paths in society.

Religion. Any system of belief that holds that there is a superior being or God, and meaningful, assigned purpose for human life. References to 'religion' are usually interchangeable with 'faith tradition'.

Ritual. A solemn, prescribed, and symbolic action carried out in a religious ceremony or act of devotion.

Sacred. Any thing or any place connected with The Divine. In a sense, everything and every place is sacred. However, it's common for members of a faith community to formally declare or *consecrate* what they deem to be sacred.

Sacrament. A rite considered by Christians to involve the blessing of divine grace.

Salvation. Deliverance from separation from God. In Christianity, Salvation refers to the forgiveness of sins and restoration of a believer to being in communion with God. More generally, the concept refers to escaping the cycle of death and rebirth and persistence of the ego's belief in its own invincibility.

Samsara. The continuing cycle of death and rebirth to which those who have not achieved nirvana are bound.

Sangha. A supportive community of believers who share a common faith.

Schism. A division between formerly united bodies within a faith tradition, usually caused by doctrinal or other differences of belief. The *Great Schism*, or break in communion between the Eastern Orthodox and Catholic Churches, is one example.

Scripture. Writing that is held to be divinely inspired. In most traditions, many scriptures that have been judged to be important teachings have been assembled into canons of books or texts intended for common reading and study.

Self. When spelled with a capital 'S' (Self), refers to the true essence of an individual, which is divine. This contrasts with the 'self' (lower case 's') that is governed by the ego, viewing itself as being independent of others and detached from God.

Soul. The non-material essence of a human being that is distinct from the Spirit, which embraces all life.

Spirit. The non-material Source of life that gives breath to every living thing. Note: Some use the terms 'Spirit' and 'Soul' interchangeably, although that usage is not how they are intended in this text.

Spiritual. A person who believes that human beings have a non-material being, as well as one that can be described regarding the physical body and nervous system. Individuals who describe themselves as being 'spiritual' usually follow a faith tradition or at least are open to accepting the possibility of the existence of God.

Spirituality. Being in connection with the inner life and concerns about The Divine or supernatural. Wayne Teasdale offers the following definition: "Spirituality is a way of life that affects and includes every moment of existence. It is at once a contemplative attitude, a disposition to a life of depth, and the search for ultimate meaning, direction, in belonging" (*The Mystic Heart: Discovering a Universal Spirituality in the World's Religions* by Wayne Teasdale, 1999, New World Library, California, p17).

The Big Six. Umbrella terms for the six major faith traditions that are widely practiced in multiple regions of the World, as measured by membership: Buddhism, Christianity, Hinduism, Islam, Judaism, Sikhism.

Theism. Belief in God (or gods) as the Creator and Sustainer of the Universe.

Bibliography

A Global Guide to Interfaith: Reflections from Around the World by Sandy Bharat and Jael Bharat, 2007, O Books

A History Of God by Karen Armstrong, 1999, Vintage

A Religion of One's Own: A Guide to Creating a Personal Spirituality in a Secular World by Thomas Moore, 2015 (reprint edition), Gotham Books

Ecumenism: A Guide for the Perplexed (Guides for the Perplexed) by R. David Nelson and Charles Raith, 2017, Bloomsbury T&T Clark

Faith, Hope and Love: Interfaith Engagement as Practical Theology by Ray Gaston, 2017, SCM Press

God is a Great Underground River: Articles, Essays & Homilies on Interfaith Spirituality by John R. Mabry, 2014 (second edition), Apocryphile Press

Interfaith Alternative: Embracing Spiritual Diversity by Rev. Steven Greenebaum, 2012, New Society Publishers

Interfaith Dialoque at the Grass Roots by Rebecca Kratz Mays, Ed., 2009, Ecumenical Press

Interfaith Theology: A Reader (One World) by Dan Cohn-Sherbok, Ed., 2001, Oneworld Publications

Living Buddha, Living Christ by Thich Nhat Hanh, 1996, Rider

Noticing the Divine: An Introduction to Interfaith Spiritual Guidance (Spiritual Directors International Books) by John Mabry, 2007, Morehouse Publishing

One River, Many Wells: Wisdom Springing from Global Faiths by Matthew Fox, 2004, Tarcherperigee

Participatory Spirituality: A Farewell to Authoritarian Religion by John Heron, 2010, lulu.com

Picturing God: How to Conceive and Relate to the Divine (An Anthology) by Clive Johnson, 2015, Labyrinthe Press

Pluralism in the World Religions: A Short Introduction by Harold Coward, 2000, One World, Oxford

Practical Interfaith: How to Find Our Common Humanity as We Celebrate Diversity by Rev. Steven Greenebaum, 2014, SkyLight Paths Publishing

Problems of Religious Pluralism by John Hick, 1994 (reprint), Palgrave Macmillan, London

Sourcebook of the World's Religions: An Interfaith Guide to Religion and Spirituality by Joel Beversluis, 2000 (third revised edition), New World Library

Spirituality: A Very Short Introduction (Very Short Introductions) by Philip Sheldrake, 2012, Oxford University Press, Oxford

The Contemporary Guide to Modern Spirituality by Michael A. Winn, 2016, XLIBRIS

The Interfaith Imperative: Religion, Dialogue, and Reality by Ross Thompson, 2017, Cascade Books

The Interfaith Movement (Temple Tracts Book 5) by Charlotte Dando, Philip Lewis, Chris Baker, (Eds.), 2015, William Temple Foundation

The Interfaith Prayer Book: New Expanded Edition by Ted Brownstein, 2014 (second edition), Lake Worth Interfaith Network

The Message That Comes From Everywhere: Exploring The Common Core of the World's Religions by Gary L. Beckwith, 2015, The Harmony Institute

The Mystic Heart: Discovering a Universal Spirituality in the World's Religions by Wayne Teasdale, 2001, New World Library

The Myth of Religious Superiority: A Multifaith Exploration by Paul F., Knitter, Ed., 2005, Orbis Books

The Perennial Philosophy by Aldous Huxley 2009 (reprint), Harper Perennial

The Power Of Modern Spirituality: How to Live a Life of Compassion and Personal Fulfilment by William Bloom, 2011, Piaktus

The Underlying Religion: An Introduction to the Perennial Philosophy by Martin Lings and Clinton Minnaar (eds.), 2007, World Wisdom Inc., Bloomington, Indiana

The Varieties of Religious Experience: A Study in Human Nature by William James, 2002 (new edition), Random House Inc.

The World's Religions by Huston Smith, 2009 (second edition), HarperOne

Waking Up: A Guide to Spirituality Without Religion by Sam Harris, 2015 (reprint edition), Simon & Schuster

Walking on Water: Reaching God in Our Time (Columba Classics) by Anthony de Mello, 2014, Columba Press

Without Buddha I Could Not be a Christian by Paul F. Knitter 2013 (reprint) Oneworld Publications

Journals

Faith Initiative Magazine. www.faithinitiative.co.uk. Provides coverage on matters relating to interfaith relations.

Interreligious Insight. www.worldfaiths.org. Thought pieces and perspectives from researchers, religious leaders, and activists. Journal of the World Congress of Faiths.

Journal of Ecumenical Studies. www.dialogueinstitute.org. Peer-reviewed journal that encourages dialogue among Christian denominations.

Religion & Ethics Newsweekly. www.pbs.org/wnet/religionandethics. Religious news coverage from around the world.

The Journal of Inter-Religious Dialogue. www.irdialogue.org. Exchange of views of scholars from different faith traditions.

The Revealer. www.wp.nyu.edu/therevealer. Daily review of religious press stories.

DVD's

Beyond Borders: Stories of Interfaith Friendship, Film Movement

Interfaith Encounters, Krishna Store

The Interfaith Dialogue (His Holiness The Dalai Lama), Friends of Tibet

Clive Johnson

The Interfaith Resources Guide

Movements and Initiatives

Canadian Interfaith Conversation. Brings together representatives of multiple faith communities and organizations, with a belief that people of faith can contribute positively for the benefit of all in Canadian society. www.interfaithconversation.ca (Canada)

Center for Interreligious Understanding. Offers educational programs relating to shared faith values and interfaith tolerance. www.ciunow.org

Ecumenical Peace Institute. Interfaith educational and activist group working for peace. www.peacehost.net/EPI-Calc

Edinburgh International Centre for Spirituality and Peace. Hosts an annual Edinburgh International Festival of Middle Eastern Spirituality and Peace, bringing together people from a wide range of spiritual backgrounds in acts of common worship and spiritual practice. www.mesp.org.uk (Scotland)

Inter Faith Week. A programme of the Inter Faith Network for the UK. www.interfaithweek.org (UK)

Inter-Religious Federation for World Peace. Includes a range of inter-religious councils, serving municipalities, nations, regions, and the United Nations. IRFWP councils comprise representatives and scholars from all world religions, who consult and collaborate to advise and guide social, political, and economic leaders. www.irfwp.org

Interfaith Alliance. National, non-partisan advocacy for interfaith tolerance. www.interfaithalliance.org (USA)

Interfaith Scotland. Promotes and facilitates cross-faith community engagement through dialogue and education. www.interfaithscotland.org (Scotland)

Interfaith Voices for Peace and Justice. A large network, offering links to over 800 faith-based and other organizations that are active in seeking peace. www.interspirit.net/ifv.cfm

Interfaith Youth Core. Provides resources and hosts events for young people focused on living out shared values such as hospitality and care for the Earth. www.ifyc.org

International Association for Religious Freedom (IARF). Consultant to the United Nations, working to preserve the human right to freedom of religion. www.iarf.net

One Spirit Alliance. Facilitates networking between faith communities. www.onespiritalliance.net

Parliament of the World's Religions. Seeks to cultivate harmony among the world's faith communities through dialogue and education. ww.parliamentofreligions.org

Regional Interfaith Network. Encourages interfaith dialogue and cooperation in Australia and the Asia-Pacific region. www.regionalinterfaith.org.au (Australia/Asia Pacific)

Religions for Peace (Australia). A large community-based organization working for inter-religious harmony. www.religionsforpeaceaustralia.org.au (Australia)

Religions for Peace. Supports inter-religious action and dialogue for peace. www.rfp.org (Global, with regional organisations)

Religious Harmony Foundation. Educational and support organisation, aiming to bring harmony among peoples of different religions, castes, and creeds. www.religiousharmony.org (India/Global)

The Inter Faith Network for the UK. Promotes understanding and cooperation between organisations and people of different faiths. Offers a wide range of free online resources for planning interfaith events (see www.interfaith.org.uk/resources/publications). www.interfaith.org.uk

The National Interfaith Council of South Africa (NICSA). Comprises all faith-based organizations in South Africa. Encourages interfaith dialogue and cooperation, and promotes interventions aimed at bringing about social harmony. www.nicsa.org.za (South Africa)

The NZ Interfaith Group. An affiliation of interfaith groups active in different parts of New Zealand. www.interfaith.org.nz (New Zealand)

The Pluralism Project. Harvard University project to document religious pluralism in the USA. www.pluralism.org (USA)

The Religious Freedom Center of the Newseum Institute. A nonpartisan initiative focused on educating the public about the religious liberty principles that are enshrined in the First Amendment. www.ReligiousFreedomCenter.org (USA)

United Religions Initiative. Promotes enduring, daily interfaith cooperation, opposing religiously motivated violence and aimed at creating cultures of peace, justice and healing for the Earth and all living beings. www.uri.org

World Congress of Faiths (WCF). Organises events and debates aimed at developing a better understanding, co-operation and respect among people of different faiths. www.worldfaiths.org (UK)

Online forums, blogs, and social media

www.interfaith.org/community. Large community offering a wide range of discussion forums relating to matters of faith and interfaith.

www.parliamentofreligions.org/forums. Varied discussion forums hosted by the Parliament of the World's Religions.

YouTube and online videos

www.interfaithconnections.squarespace.com. *Interfaith Connections* TV Show.

www.parliamentofreligions.org/videos. Large collection of videos of events hosted by the Parliament of the World's Religions.

www.uri.org. Offers a range of videos relating to the work of the United Religions Initiative.

www.worldfaith.org. Project Interfaith USA. YouTube video-sharing project, RavelUnravel. Allows individuals to share personal religious stories.

Podcasts

www.abc.net.au/radionational/programs/spiritofthings/aspire-to-interfaith/7780936. *The Spirit of Things*, ABC Radio National, 'Aspire to Interfaith.' Explores an initiative to create a new centre for interfaith.

www.abc.net.au/radionational/programs/spiritofthings/interfacing-with-interfaith/2960508. *The Spirit of Things*, ABC Radio National, 'Interfacing with Interfaith.' Discusses the consequences of interfaith dialogue between two Jews, two Catholics and two Muslims.

www.bbc.co.uk/programmes/b08j9z6j. *Beyond Belief*, BBC. Discussion considering interfaith worship.

www.bbc.co.uk/programmes/p002vsn4. *Heart and Soul*, BBC. Explores individual approaches to spirituality from around the world.

www.celebrateradio.com. *Celebrate Radio*. Podcasts published by the United Religions Initiative.

www.hosts.blogtalkradio.com/openmindsopenhearts. Interfaith radio show.

www.huffingtonpost.com/topic/all-together-podcast. *All Together*, Huffpost. Archive of episodes taking varied explorations of faith and spirituality, including interfaith perspectives.

www.interfaithradio.org. *Interfaith Radio*. Public radio news magazine.

www.ncronline.org/news/without-buddha-i-could-not-be-christian-paul-knitter. N*ational Catholic Reporter* podcast: 'Without Buddha I Could Not Be a Christian: Paul Knitter,' 7 July 2010.

www.onbeing.org. *On Being with Krista Tippett*. On Being's archive provides a growing number of previously broadcast podcasts concerning interfaith and pluralism.

Ministry Training

www.allfaithsseminary.org All Faiths Seminary International (USA)

www.allpathsdivinityschool.org All Paths Divinity School (USA)

www.interfaithfoundation.org OneSpirit Interfaith Foundation (UK)

www.new-seminary.com The New Seminary (USA)

www.onespiritinterfaith.org One Spirit Learning Alliance (USA)

Note: Most US-based seminaries offer distance learning programs for students of any nationality.

Clive Johnson

ACKNOWLEDGEMENTS

My thanks are due to all the teachers, supporters, and fellow walkers who have helped me on my interfaith journey; to Content Writer for her excellent proof reading and editing; and to The Great Divine–The One Who is both beyond and fully within everything that associates with the name 'interfaith.'

Clive Johnson

ABOUT THE AUTHOR

Clive Johnson is a life-long spiritual seeker, interfaith minister, and retreat host. This is his ninth book.

www.clivejohnson.info
www.clivejohnsonministry.com

ALSO BY CLIVE JOHNSON:

Picturing God: How to conceive and relate to the Divine (An Anthology)
Fairy Stories & Fairy Stories: Traditional tales for children, Contemporary tales for adults
Arabian Nights & Arabian Nights: Traditional tales from a thousand and one nights, Contemporary tales for adults
Labyrinth A–Ω: An Introduction to the How, What and Why of Labyrinths and Labyrinth Walking
The Complete Guide to Visioning: How to discover, shape and realize your vision

Coming soon:

Modern Spirituality for the Non-religious
Ceremonies for One
Spiritual Practice A–Ω

Clive Johnson

Printed in Great Britain
by Amazon